MICROSOFT ONEDRIVE MADE EASY

Cloud Storage & Backup Simplified

By James Bernstein

Printed in the United States of America

Bernstein, James
Box Made Easy
Part of the Productivity Apps Made Easy series

For more information on reproducing sections of this book or sales of this book,
go to **www.madeeasybookseries.com**

Contents

Introduction

With everything being done online these days, it seems as though you need to know how to master a multitude of technologies just to get your work done. We are expected to know how to use email, texting, social media, cloud-based office productivity services, smartphone apps and so on.

Not too long ago (depending on who you ask), when we wanted to share files and collaborate with our peers, we would have to send files back and forth via email and hope that we were working on the latest version of the file. Doing this would also get complicated when we had many people we were working with on a project at the same time.

Another option was to use what is known as an FTP (File Transfer Protocol) site to store and share files. But this takes some technical skills to set up, and you also need your own server to store these files on. These are still in use today by businesses but are not practical for the home or small business user.

Fortunately, today we have many options as to where we can store and share our files and it seems like we are almost getting pressured into using these services. For example, when you get a new computer running Windows, it will automatically configure their online storage platform called OneDrive and you may not even notice that it is up and running. And if you have a Google\Gmail account, you automatically get access to their Google Drive service whether you plan on using it or not!

The goal of this book is to get you up and running with Microsoft OneDrive and comfortable with the interface when it comes to uploading and downloading files and folders. I will also be going over how to share and collaborate with other OneDrive and non-OneDrive users.

Once you understand the main concept of how OneDrive and other cloud storage services work, it will make the experience that much easier and also prepare you to use other online storage services at the same time since not everyone uses OneDrive for their cloud storage needs. So, on that note, let's head to the cloud!

Chapter 1 – What is OneDrive?

Before showing you how to use OneDrive, I would like to spend a little time going over what exactly it is and what you will expect to see when you first start using it. I will be working with the free account that anyone with a Microsoft account has access to as well as a Microsoft 365 account that offers extra storage and other features.

Cloud Storage Overview

In order to get an understanding of what exactly OneDrive does, you should first have an idea of the concept of cloud storage. You are probably used to storing your files and folders on your hard drive and maybe use a removable USB hard drive or flash drive to back up your files or transfer them between computers.

Doing things this way is fine for many people but if you are going to be sharing your files with others or want a way to backup important files offsite, then using cloud storage might be the solution you need.

The term cloud storage refers to storing your files on servers that are located at other locations around the country, or even around the world. Then when you access your files and folders, you do so via a web browser or client software over the internet. This allows you to work on your files remotely or download them to your local computer and then sync them back with the server when you save them again.

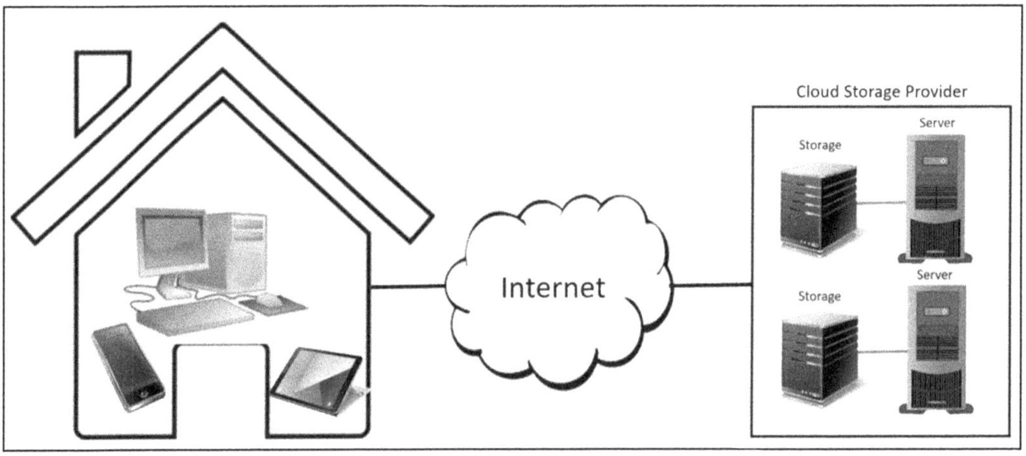

Figure 1.1

Types of Cloud Storage

There are four main types of cloud storage typically in use today. I will be focusing on just one of them, but I wanted to go over the others, so you have an idea of what is available out there.

- **Personal Cloud Storage** – This is what we will be focusing on for the most part and is mainly used to store a user's personal data online, allowing them to access it from anywhere that they have an Internet connection and a device capable of accessing their data. This can be done via a desktop computer, laptop, smartphone, or tablet, and all you need to do is sign into your account and you are off and running.

- **Public Cloud Storage** – This is used when a company doesn't have its own cloud storage resources and all of the infrastructure for the storage is managed off-site by another company which also takes care of all aspects of the cloud storage, including making sure it's available all the time and also backed up. Public Cloud Storage providers will store data from many customers all at the same location.

- **Private Cloud Storage** — If a company wants to utilize cloud storage and have it located within their own data center but still be managed by a third party, then they can take the private route. This is common when the data is private or confidential and the company needs to know where it is at all times.

- **Hybrid Cloud Storage** — Hybrid Cloud Storage is a combination of Public and Private Cloud Storage where a company will have its critical data stored at its own location while having less important data stored at the cloud provider's location.

Benefits of Cloud Storage

Not all cloud storage is the same, so the benefits will vary based on the type you choose. Since we are only dealing with the personal type, that is what I will be focusing on going forward.

I have many clients that I do work for, and one thing that is common among a lot of them is the lack of backups. (That is until I force them to start doing them!) If you are like most people, then you have many (or even too many) pictures on your computer as well as music and documents that you would be very upset about losing. If you don't do a backup, then you risk a disaster if your hard drive fails or at least have the potential to spend a lot of money on a data recovery service.

Even if you do backup your data at home or at the office, there's a chance of losing it in situations involving such things as fires or floods. In fact, many companies who do their own local backups will have a service that comes by and takes their backups to a secure location offsite to ensure that they will always be safe.

For us home users having a personal backup assistant is not an option, so we are on our own to make sure we have our data securely backed up. This is where having a cloud storage account can come in handy. If you copy your important files to a location in the cloud, then they are safe there in case something happens to your computer or the location of where your computer is stored. In a worst-case scenario you can get your computer back up and running and then restore your files from your cloud backup right to your computer.

Another benefit of cloud storage is having your data available all the time, no matter where you are. Let's say you are out of town on vacation and brought your laptop or tablet with you and need to get a copy of your resume to apply for a job you want to get in on right away. If you have your data in the cloud, all you would have to do is log on to your account, download your resume, and send it off. Many times, there are options to create a link right to a specific file that you can email to someone, but I will get into that later.

Another way to use cloud storage to your benefit is when you are collaborating with other people on a team project and need to share information. Depending on what cloud provider you go with, you will usually have the option to share files and folders with other people and assign levels of permissions to those people so nobody can get away with doing something they shouldn't be doing to your files, plus it will usually show the last person who made a change to a file with the date and time.

We are all familiar with computer viruses and spyware and how they can ruin our day when they infect our computers. Some of them can even encrypt your files making them inaccessible to you forever. Plus, there's always the chance of you sending an infected file to someone else and infecting their computer. If you have a backup of your files in the cloud, then they will be safe from getting infected (assuming you have not uploaded the infected files to your cloud location).

Disadvantages of Cloud Storage

Many companies use cloud-based storage and applications to save money because they don't need to buy the hardware to support them and hire IT people to maintain them. The main downside is that if you lose your Internet connection then you lose access to your storage and programs, but for big corporations, it's rare that they have much or any downtime.

For us home users, we have the same types of choices, but on a smaller scale. Here are some of the *disadvantages* of cloud storage:

- **Dependency on the Internet** – Since you need Internet access to get to your files in the cloud, you will have to rely on your Internet service to be up. If you lose your Internet connection, then you won't be able to access your files unless you have downloaded a copy to your computer. Home users tend to not have the same reliability when it comes to their Internet connection as big companies do. That's most likely because these corporate accounts cost much more money.

- **Trusting a third party with your data** – Since you don't know *exactly* where your files are being stored and who *really* has access to them, you will have to put some trust in your cloud provider. For all you know, your files may be sitting somewhere in another country with who knows who looking at them.

- **Cost** – Many cloud storage providers will allow you to have a small amount of storage space for free with the plan of enticing you to buy more space once you fill up the free space they've provided. This can get costly if you have a lot of data since the free accounts will only hold so much.

- **Performance** – If you have a slow Internet connection or have huge files, then you will need to wait for your files to download or upload. Plus, if you are working on your smartphone using your cellular connection, it might be even slower.

For the most part, you have nothing to lose in trying out a free cloud storage provider like OneDrive, Google Drive or Dropbox to see if it is something you would like to use on a regular basis. Then you can determine if the cost is worth the advantages you get from keeping your data in the cloud, or if you don't feel comfortable using this type of service.

OneDrive Plans and Pricing

Just like with most online services, OneDrive offers a free plan as well as many subscription-based plans. These plans are broken down into Basic, Personal and Family. There are also several business plans available for corporate use.

As of this writing, there are four available plans for individual accounts and three subscription type accounts are shown in figure 1.2. As you can see, Microsoft bundles the premium OneDrive accounts with their Microsoft Office 365 subscriptions.

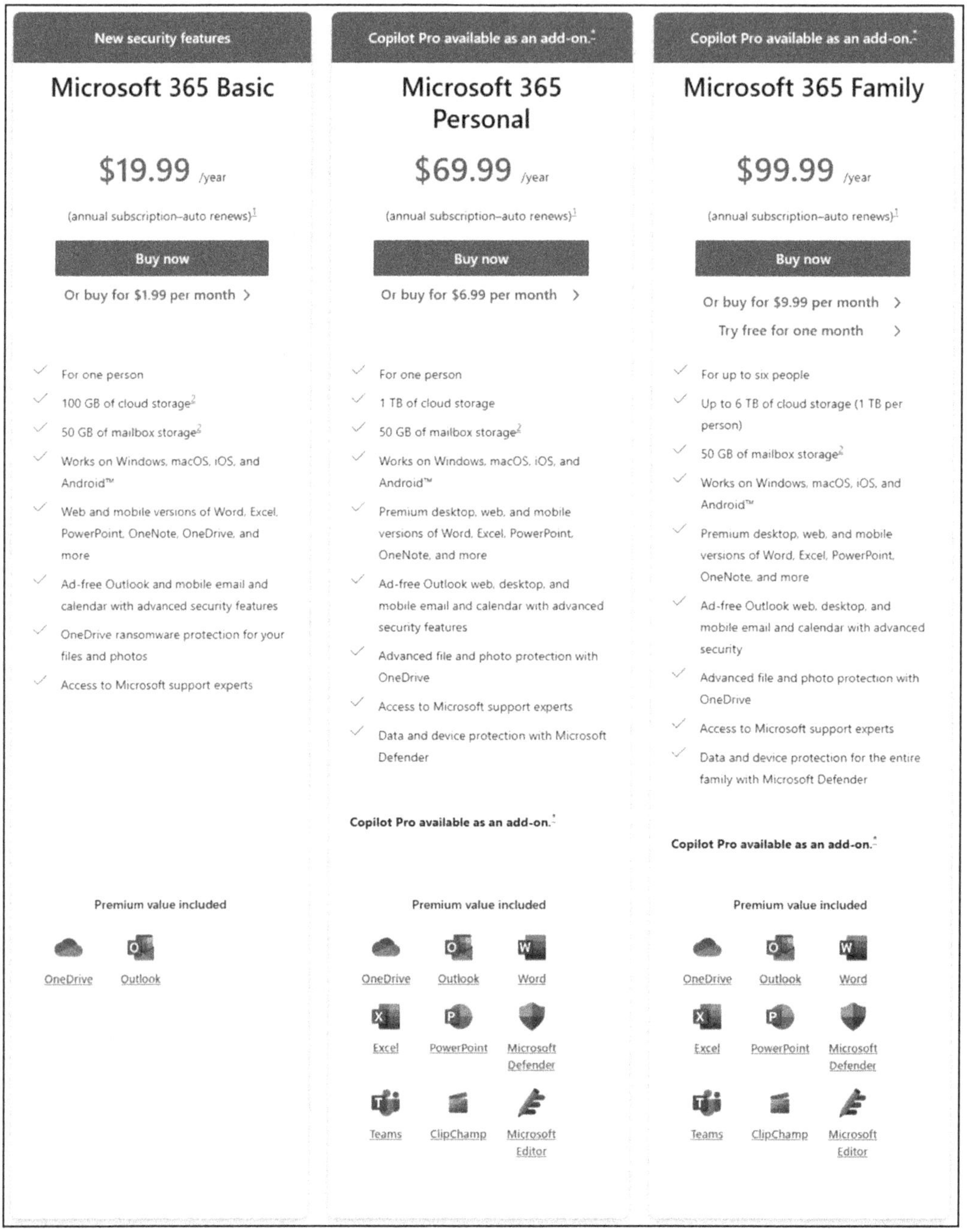

Figure 1.2

Figure 1.3 shows what features you get with the free OneDrive plan. As you can see, you get 5GB of cloud storage and 15GB of mailbox storage assuming you are using a Microsoft Email account which you don't have to have in order to use OneDrive. Unlike the subscription versions, you only get access to the web versions of the Office apps such as Word and Excel rather than the full Microsoft 365 versions that you can run on your computer.

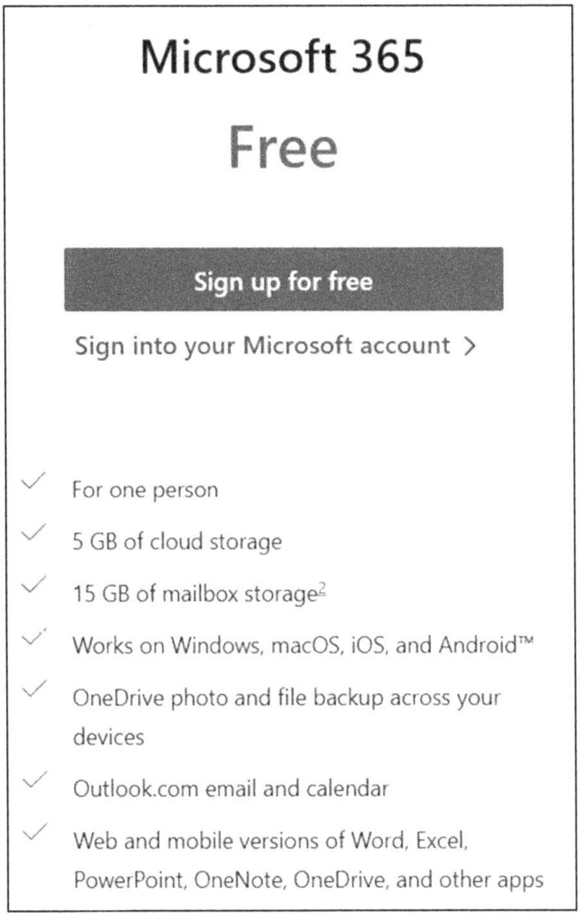

Figure 1.3

Signing Up for an Account

If you are a Windows user, then you most likely sign into Windows using an email address connected to your Microsoft account. You can use this email address to sign into the OneDrive website or you can create a new account with a different email address. If you plan on using the OneDrive desktop client (discussed in Chapter 4), you may want to use the same email address that you use for logging into your computer.

If you are not sure what email address you are using for your computer because maybe you have a PIN setup for login, you can go to the Windows settings to find the email address used for your Microsoft account.

You will find your email address in the upper left corner of the *Home* section in the Windows settings. As you can see at the bottom of Figure 1.4, there is even an option to sign into OneDrive from the settings app.

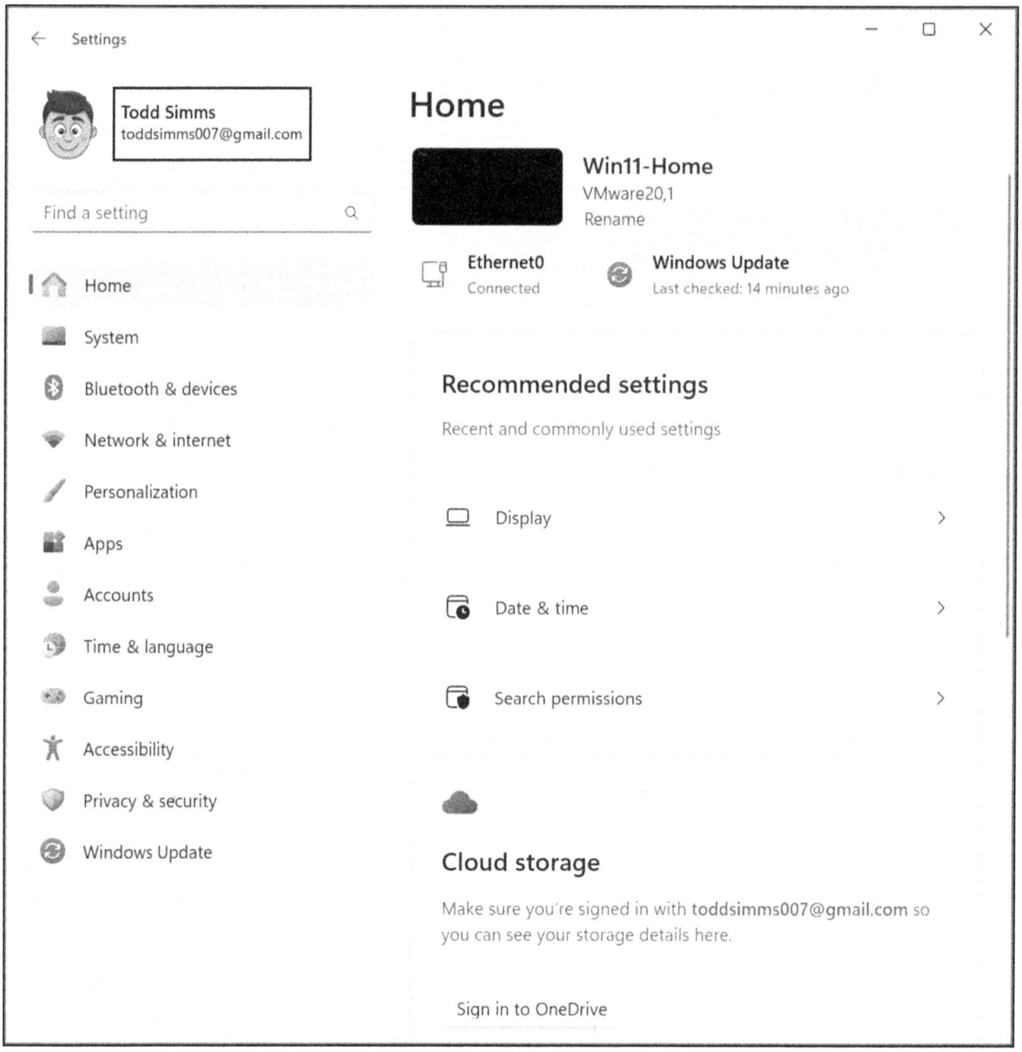

Figure 1.4

If you plan on using a different email address for your OneDrive account, you go to the OneDrive website at **https://onedrive.live.com/login/** and at the sign in screen, click on the link that says *Create one*. If you wanted to use your existing Microsoft Account, all you would need to do is type it in on the line under *Sign in* and then type your password on the next screen.

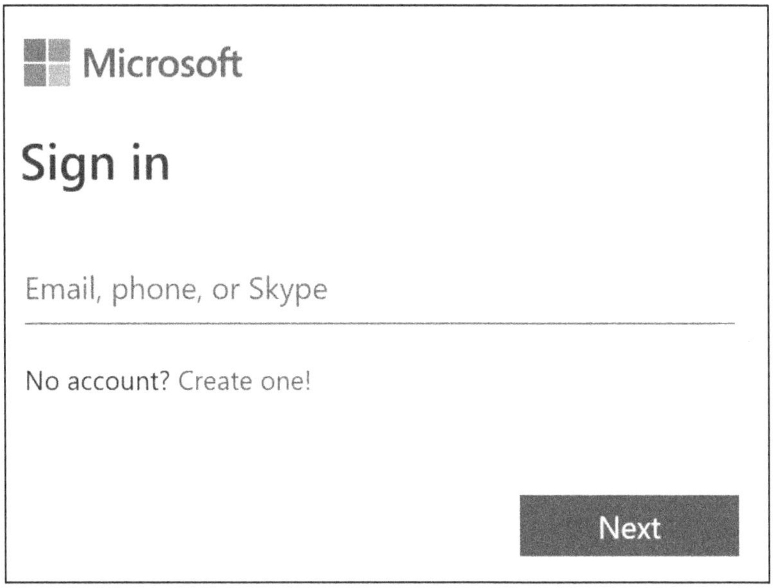

Figure 1.5

On the next screen, you can either type in an email address that you already own to use with your Microsoft\OneDrive account or click on *Get a new email address* to create a new one.

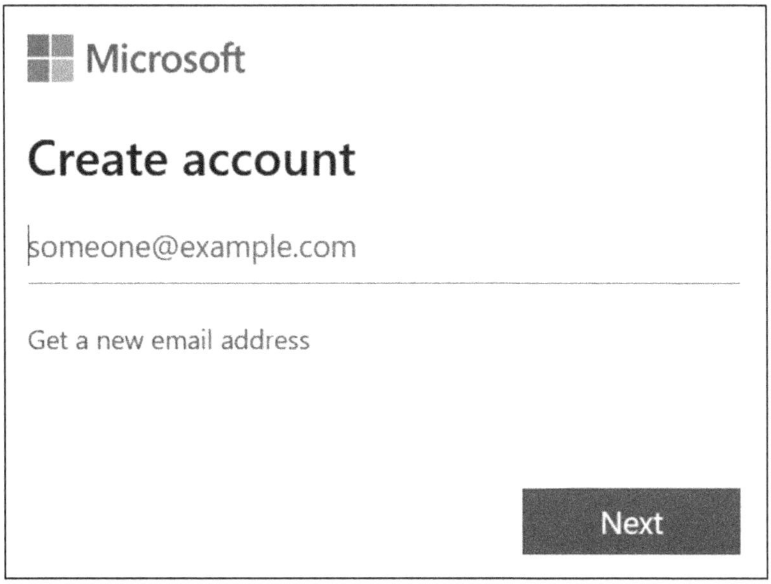

Figure 1.6

Then you would be asked to configure a password and might be asked a couple of security questions and then you will have your new Microsoft account that you can use to log into OneDrive.

The OneDrive Interface

Once You log into the OneDrive website, you will see any files and folders that you have uploaded or created. If this is your first time using OneDrive, then you will not see much there until you start adding files and folders from your computer or creating them from within OneDrive itself.

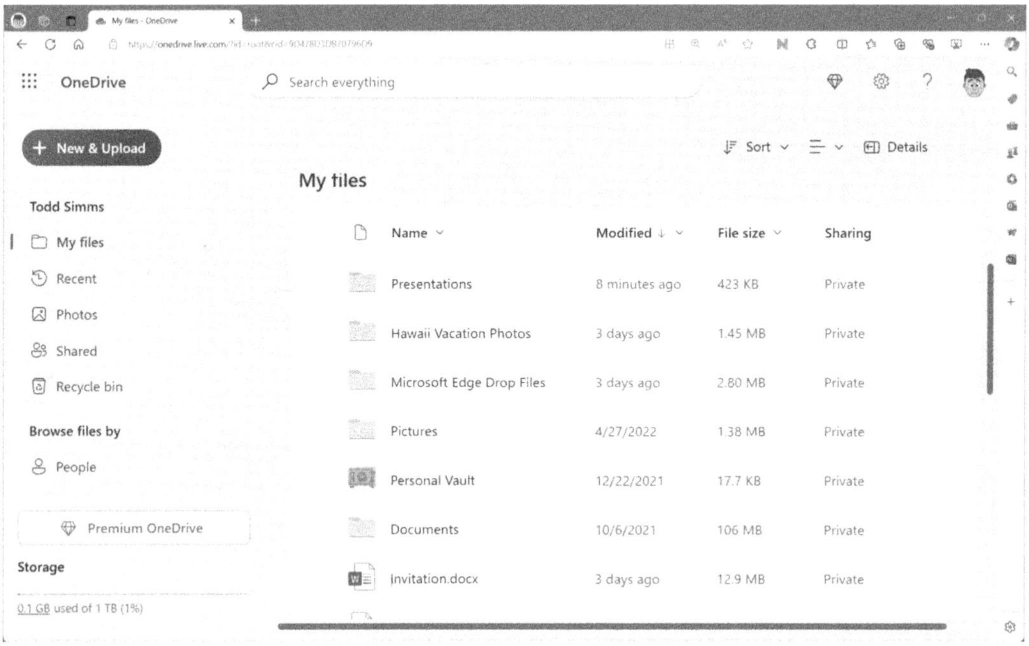

Figure 1.7

As you can see from Figure 1.7, the OneDrive interface is not too complicated and looks similar to other cloud storage platforms such as Dropbox and Google Drive.

You will have your main files and folder in the middle section of the interface and off to the left you will have some options to create new files and folders or view specific files such as photos. The left navigation panel can be "minimized" to just show icons instead of text to give you more space on the page.

At the top of the window, you will have a search box that can be used to help you find files once you get to the point where you have so many that it's hard to do manually. I will be discussing the search options in Chapter 3.

At the upper right, you will have some view options such as the ability to sort your files by name, modified date and file size. You can also change the default view from list to compact list or tiles. The tile view is shown in Figure 1.8.

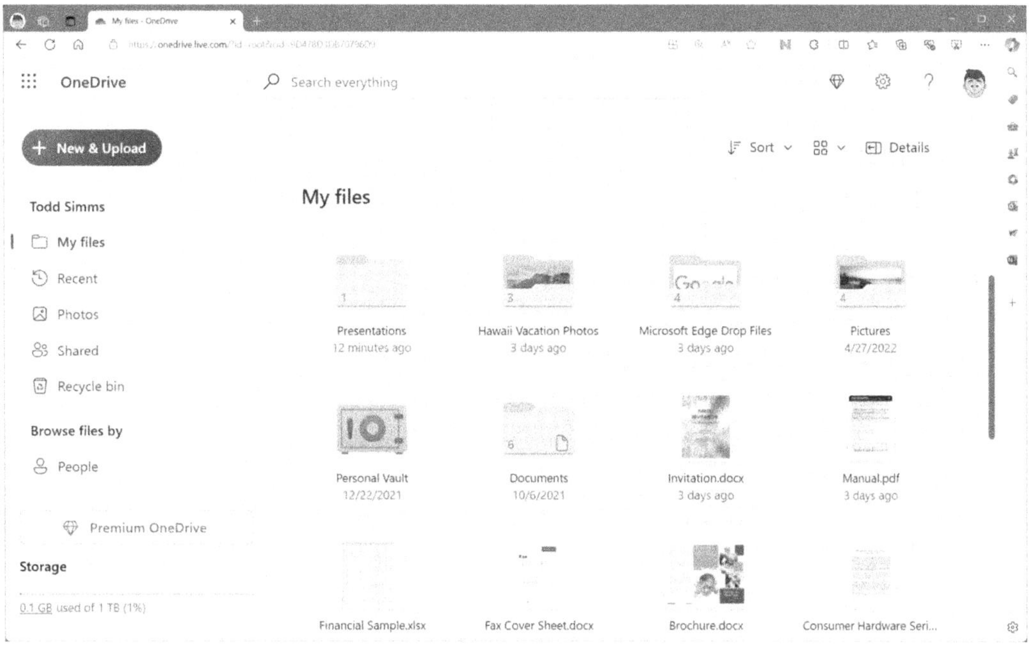

Figure 1.8

The Details pane is used to view more detailed information about your files and folders such as who they are shared with, their size, modified date, created date and so on. I will be discussing the Details pane in more detail in Chapter 3.

At the lower left, you will see how much of your total cloud storage space you have used up. This space also applies to your email account if you use a Microsoft email address such as *@outlook.com*.

Chapter 2 – Uploading & Creating Files and Folders

Since the purpose of using cloud storage services such as OneDrive is to store your files and folders in the cloud, it makes sense that you should know how to upload files and folders as well as create them from within OneDrive itself.

Uploading From Your Computer

When it comes to adding files and folders to your OneDrive online storage, you will most likely be uploading files from your computer rather than creating them within OneDrive. You can even upload files from your smartphone using the OneDrive app (discussed later in this chapter).

To upload a file or folder, you can click on the *New & Upload* button at the upper left of the OneDrive website, and from there you will want to choose either *Files upload* or *Folder upload*.

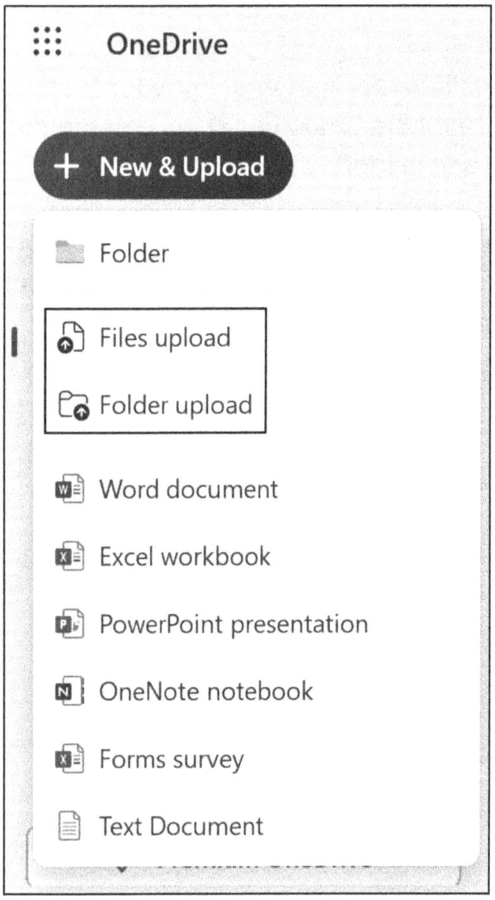

Figure 2.1

If you choose the Files upload option, you will see your files and folders but will only be able to upload files (Figure 2.2). If you choose the Folder upload option, you will only see your folders but once you choose a folder, all the files within that folder will also be uploaded.

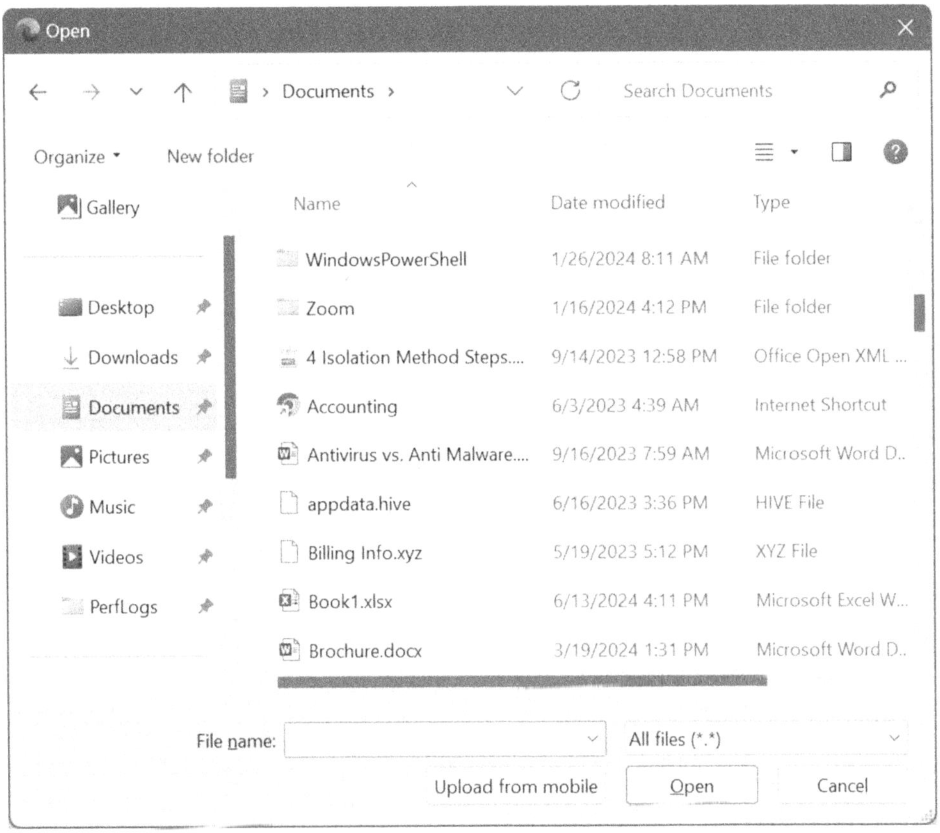

Figure 2.2

I will now upload a folder called *Confidential Files* that has several files within it as well as some subfolders.

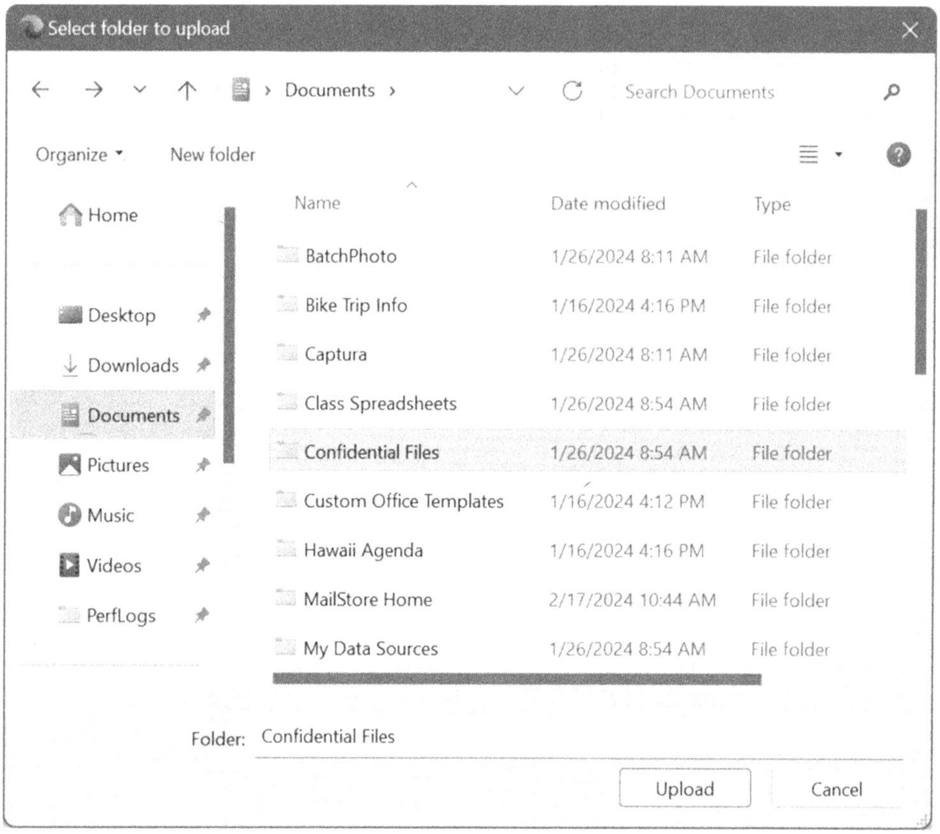

Figure 2.3

OneDrive tells me that there are 10 files within this folder and its subfolders and then I just need to click the *Upload* button to have them uploaded to the OneDrive website.

Figure 2.4

Since I am sorting my files and folders by date, my newly uploaded folder is shown at the top of the list. It even shows an indicator at the upper left of the folder name that tells me it's a newly uploaded folder.

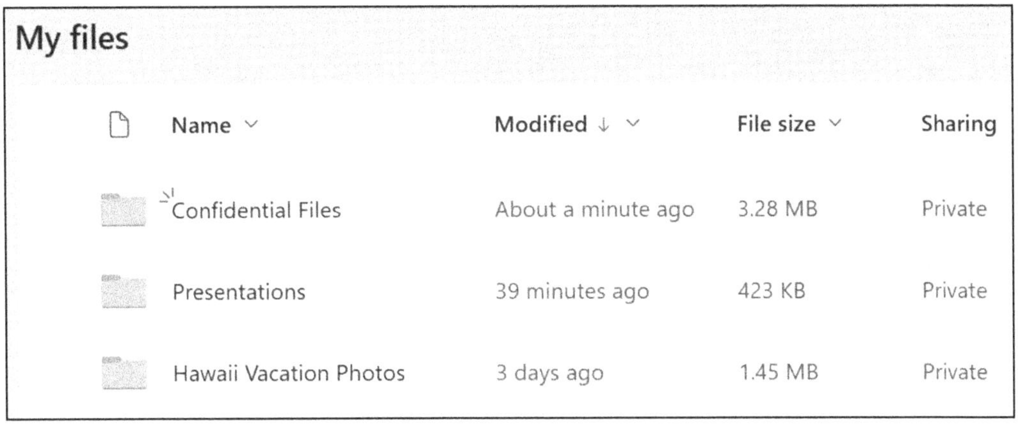

Figure 2.5

Now when I double click my newly uploaded Confidential Files folder, I can then see the files and other folders contained within this folder.

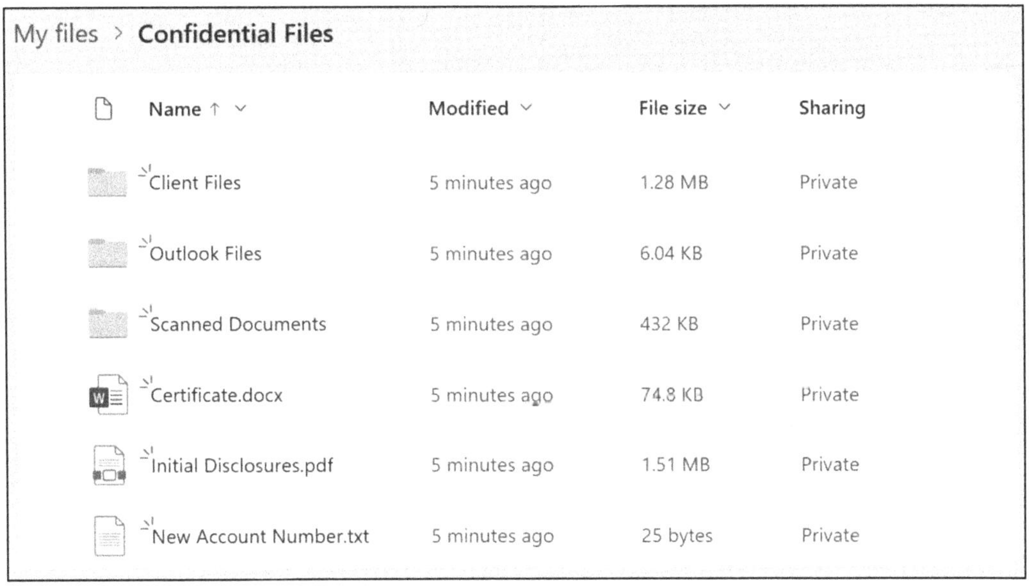

Figure 2.6

Creating Files and Folders Within OneDrive

If you are used to using Microsoft Office apps such as Word and Excel, you can easily create new documents or spreadsheets right from OneDrive itself. Then you can edit these files online from your web browser or download them to work on them on your computer.

To create a file or folder directly from OneDrive, you will need to click on the New & Upload button again and then choose your option.

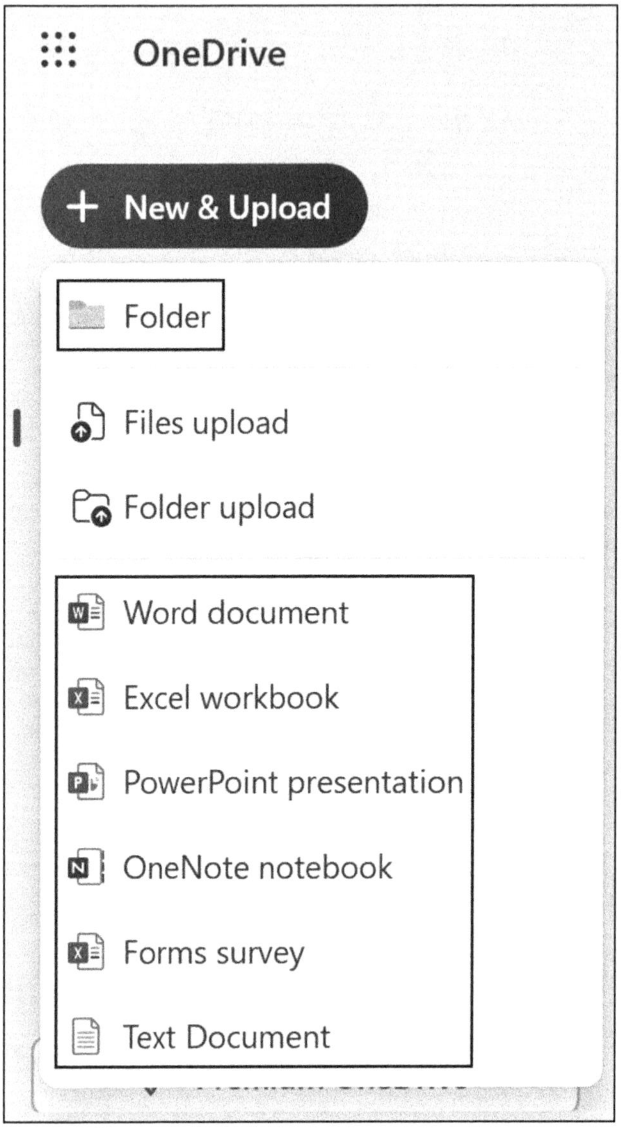

Figure 2.7

If you want to make a folder, you can click on *Folder* and then type in the name you want to use for this new folder and click on the *Create* button. I will name my new folder *Sales Reports*.

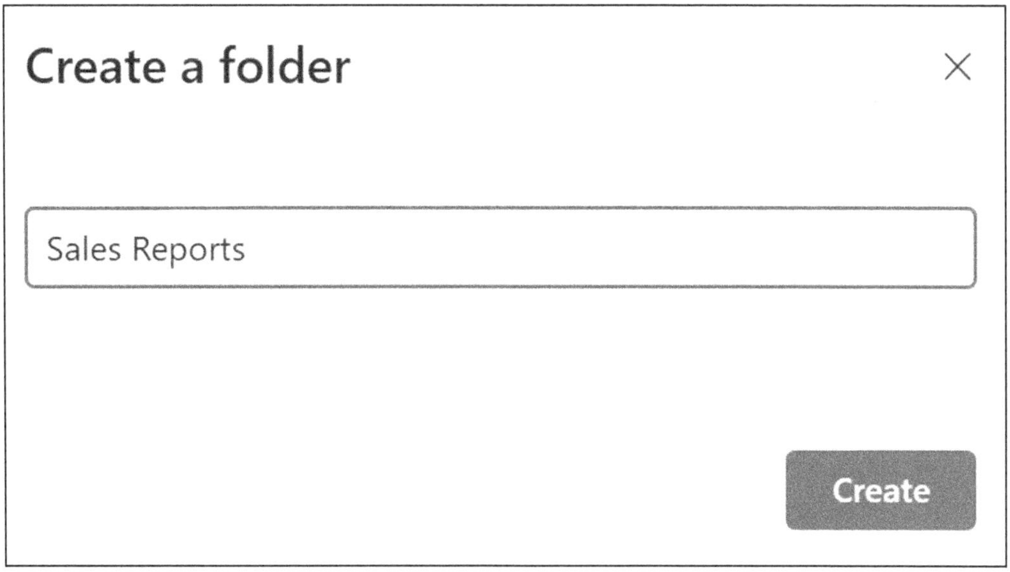

Figure 2.8

When creating a folder within OneDrive, it will create the folder in the location where you happen to be. So, for my example, I was in the main My files section so therefore it created the new Sales Report folder there.

Figure 2.9

Now I will go to my *Pictures* folder in OneDrive and create a new folder called *Vacation*.

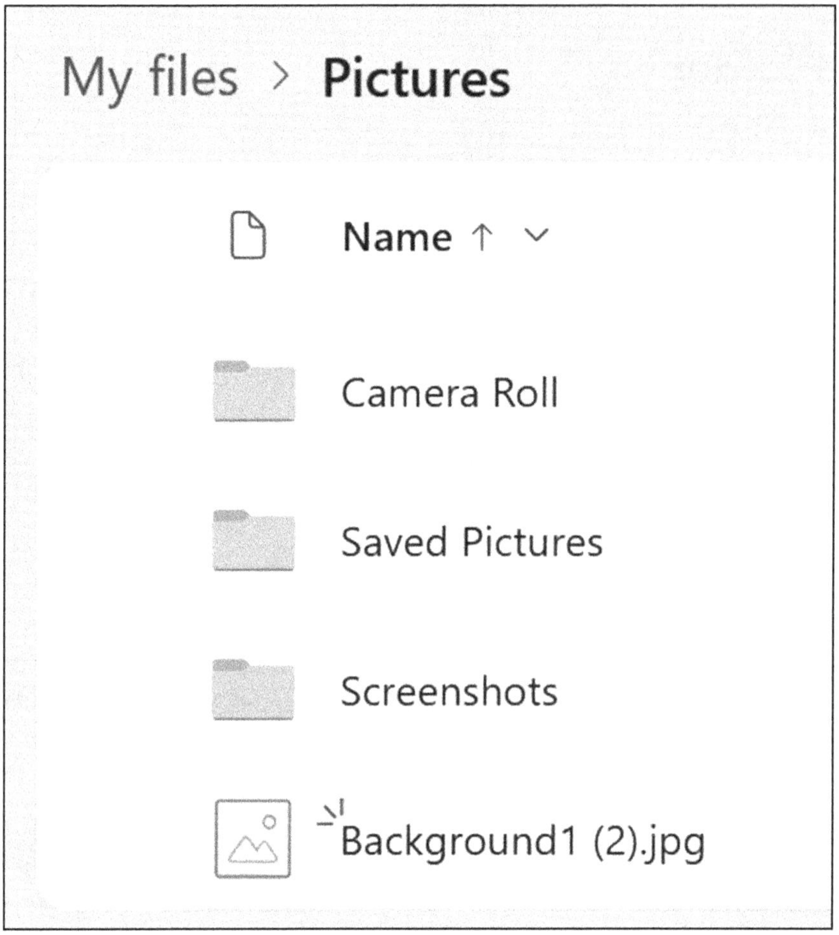

Figure 2.10

As you can see in Figure 2.11, my newly created folder called Vacation has been added as a subfolder within my Pictures folder. This will also apply to files and folders you upload from your computer.

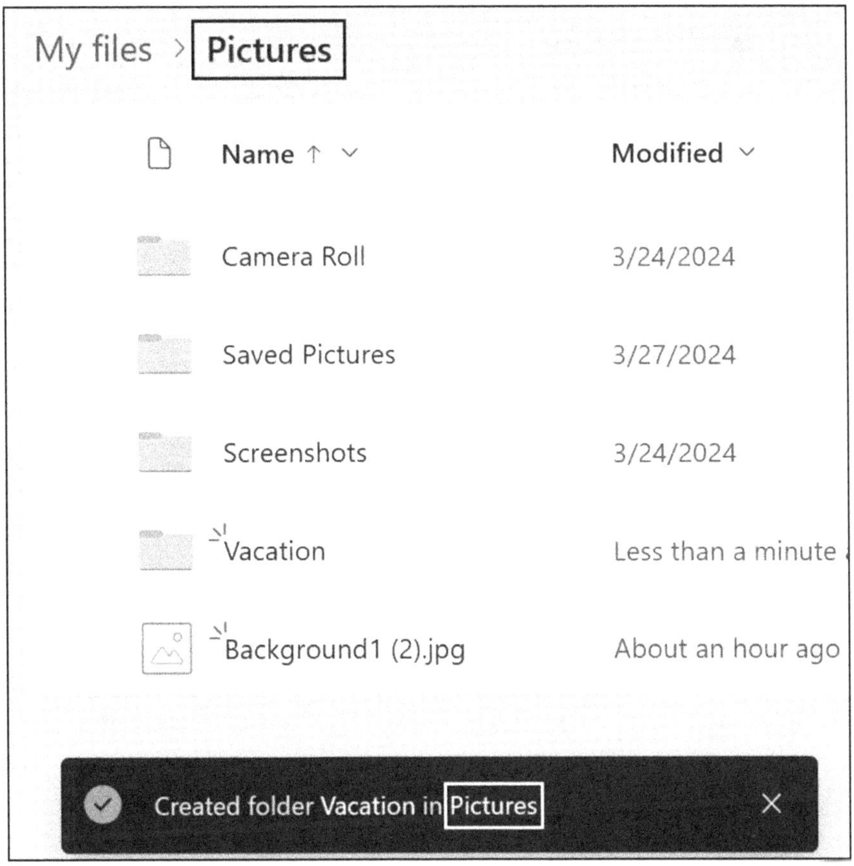

Figure 2.11

When you click on the New & Upload button, you can also create various Microsoft Office type files as well as a blank text document. I will now choose the *Word document* option and OneDrive will create a new blank document within the folder you were in when you chose the new file.

You can then start doing things such as adding text or pictures and your changes will be saved automatically as you work.

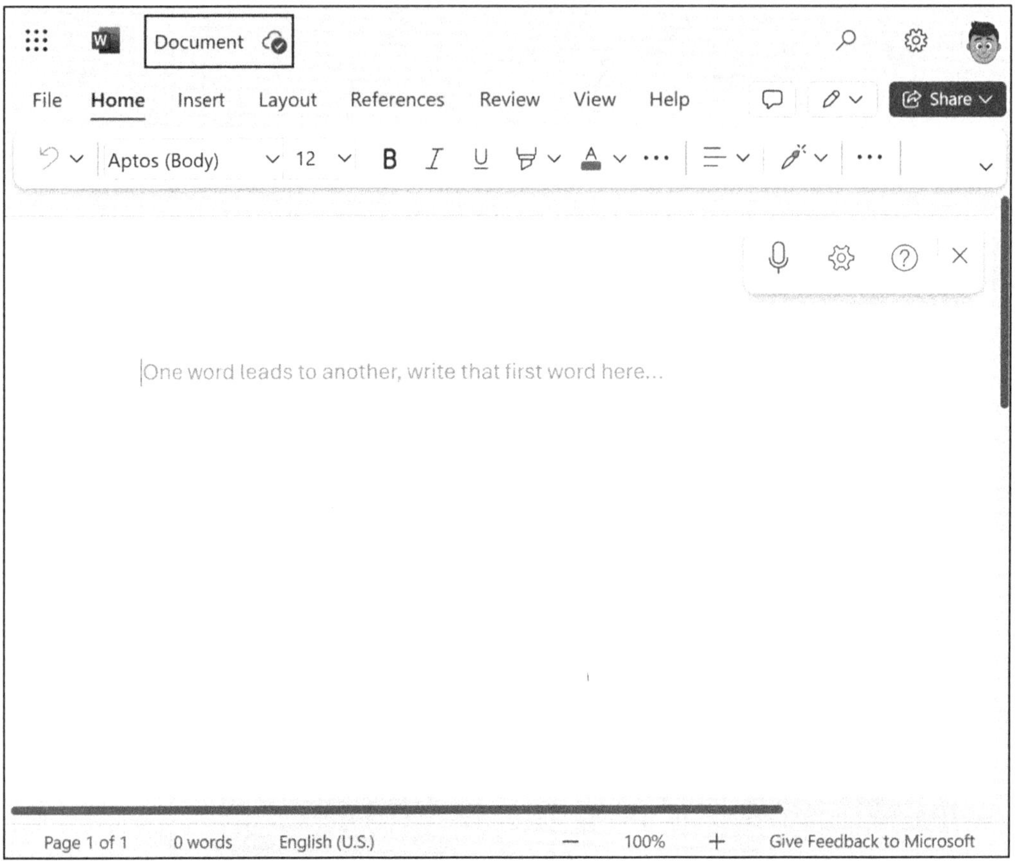

Figure 2.12

If you want to change the name of the document from the default *Document*, you can click on the word Document and type in a new name. I will name my new file *Meeting Notes*. You can also click on the cloud icon to see where your file is saved.

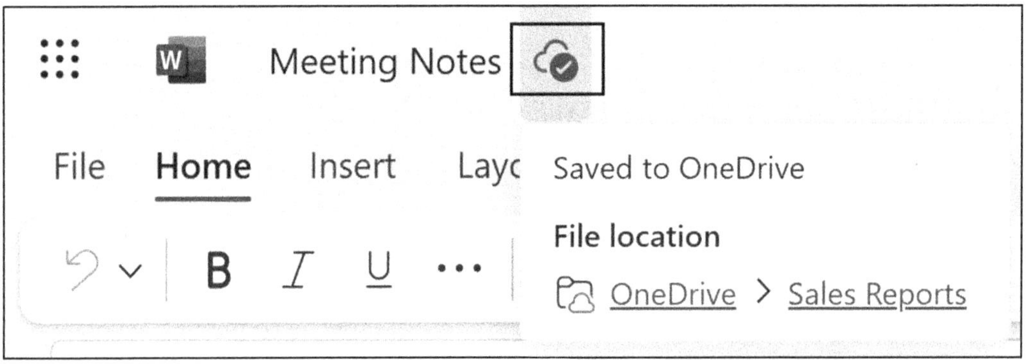

Figure 2.13

Now when I go to my Sales Reports folder, I will see my new Meeting Notes Word document.

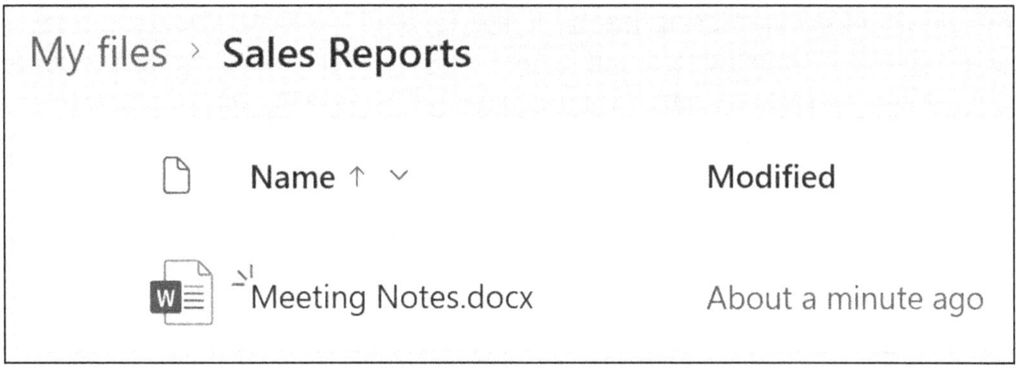

Figure 2.14

If you want to change the save location of the document, you can go to the *File* menu in Word and choose *Move File,* and then choose a new location. You can also move (and copy) files from within the OneDrive interface itself (Discussed in Chapter 3).

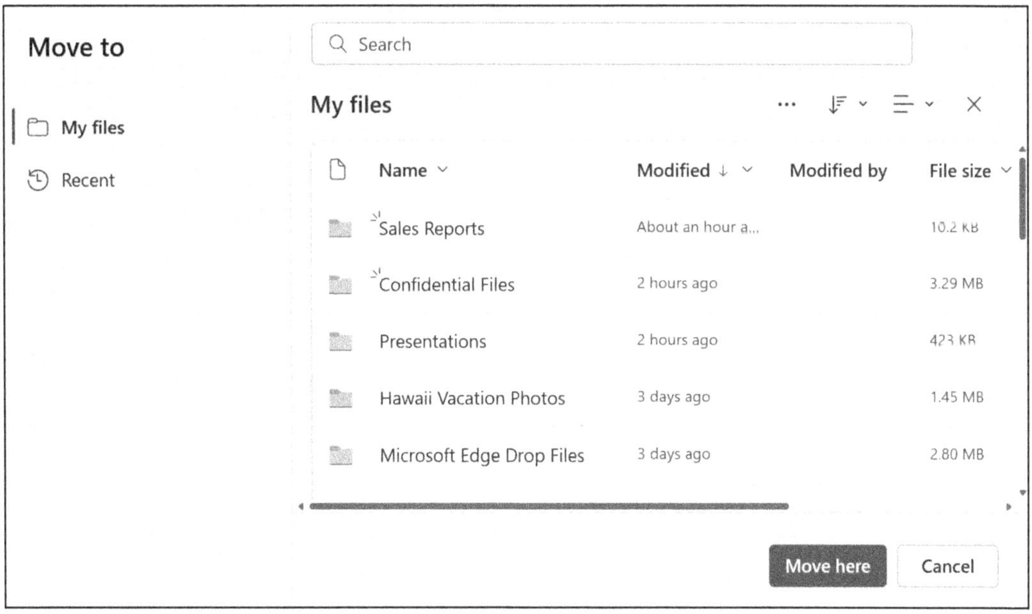

Figure 2.15

Navigating Your Folders

Once you start creating or uploading folders, you will need to know how to navigate within your folders so you can find the files that you need. When you are in a folder, you will be shown the path to that folder at the top of the list of files. Figure 2.16 shows that I am in the *ACME Docs* folder which is a subfolder of *Client Files*. Then Client Files is a subfolder of *Confidential Files*. Then finally, Confidential Files is in the root of my OneDrive in the My files section.

You may find yourself using the back and forward button on your browser to switch between your folders. But an easier way involves clicking on the folder name you want to go to right from the folder path at the top of your file list. So, if I were to click on the word Client Files, I would be taken to that folder as shown in Figure 2.17.

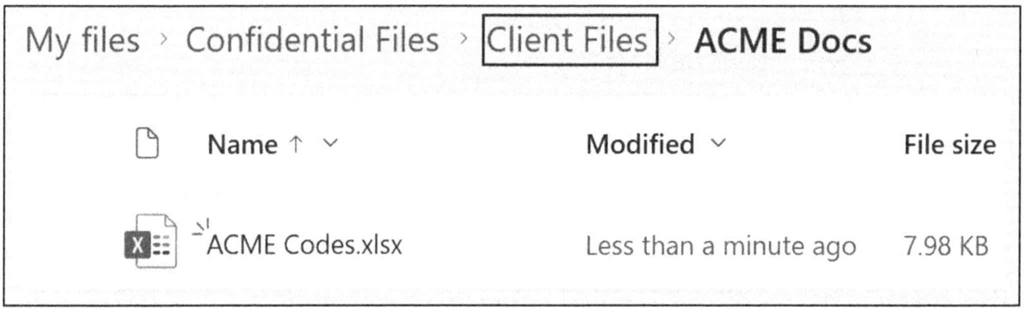

Figure 2.16

This process comes in very handy when you have a lot of subfolders, and you need to navigate between them. This will only work when going back to a folder or folders and not going forward to deeper level folders.

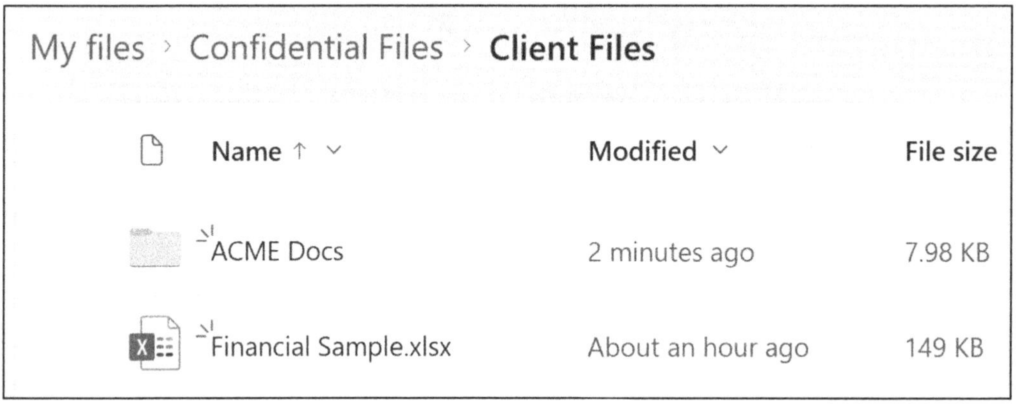

Figure 2.17

Saving Attachments from Outlook Mail to Your OneDrive Account

If you happen to have a Microsoft email account such as an outlook.com address, you can save attachments from your email directly to your OneDrive storage account.

While in your email, you can click the down arrow next to the attachment and choose the *Save to OneDrive* option.

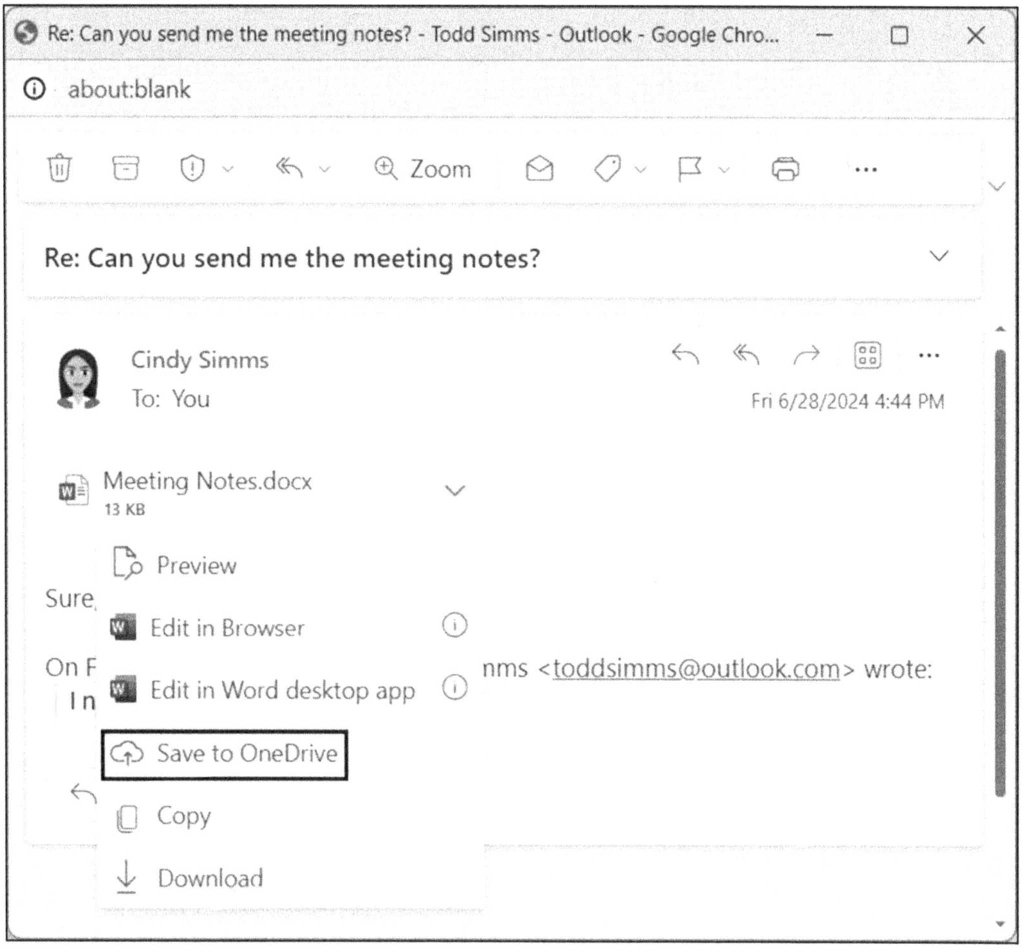

Figure 2.18

Your attachment will then be saved to the *Attachments* folder in your OneDrive account. Once you see the message that your attachment has been saved, you can then click the down arrow again and choose the *View in OneDrive* choice to see your saved files.

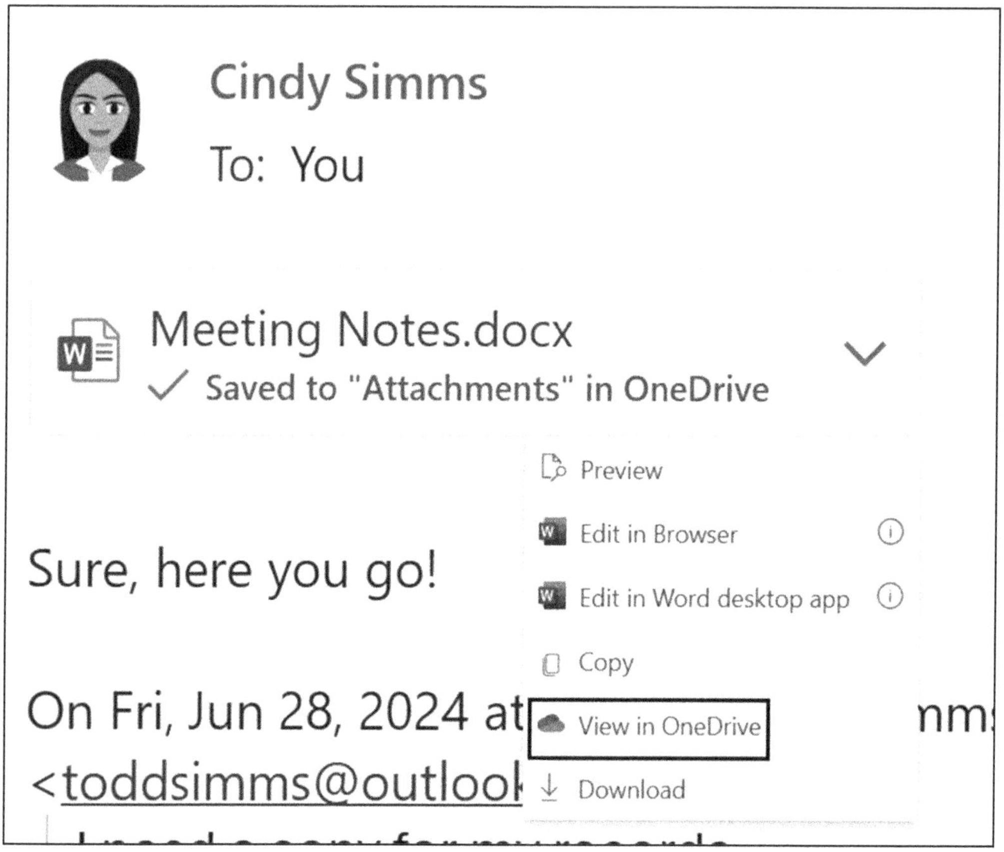

Figure 2.19

You can also simply go to your OneDrive account and find the *Attachments* folder under My files to see your saved attachments.

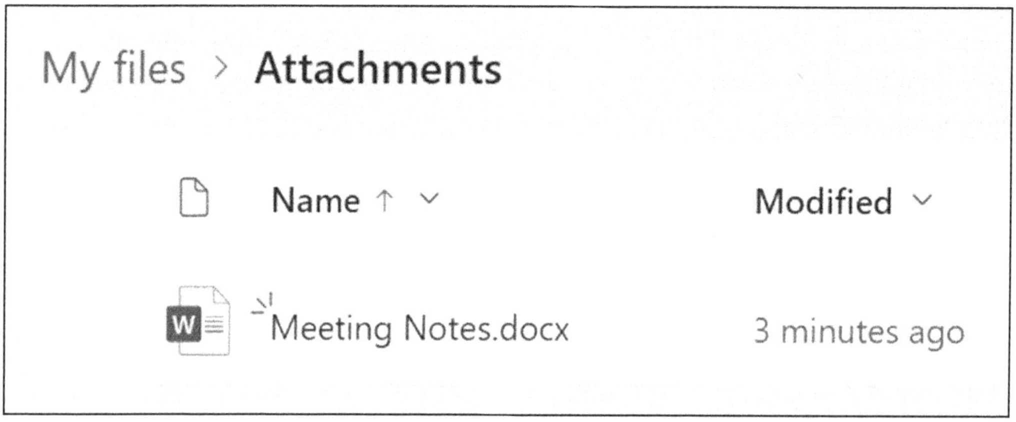

Figure 2.20

Using the OneDrive Mobile App

If you plan on being a serious OneDrive user and need access to your files at all times, you can install the OneDrive app on your smartphone or tablet. You can find the OneDrive app in the Google Play Store or the Apple App Store and install it just like you would any other app.

When you open the app the first time, you will need to log in with the email address and password that you use for your account. Then when you go to the Files section, you should see the same files and folders as you do on the OneDrive website. The images below are from an Android smartphone so if you are using an iPhone, yours may look a little different.

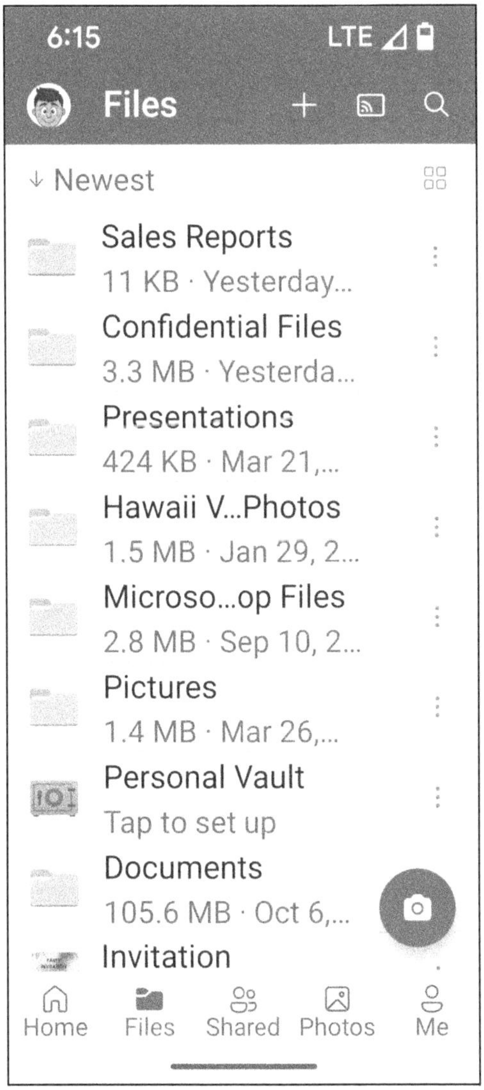

Figure 2.21

When you tap on the three vertical dots next to a file or folder, you will see similar options as you would see on the website.

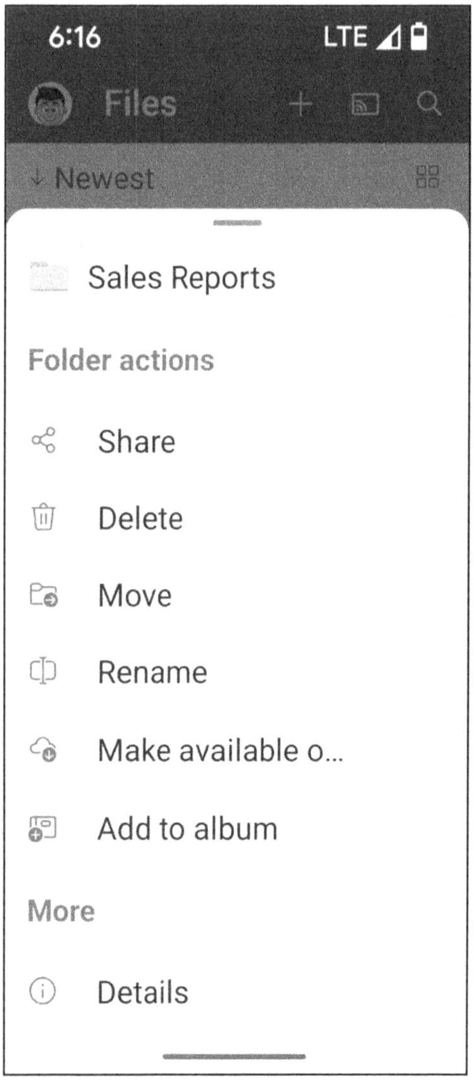

Figure 2.22

Tapping on the + button will allow you to create a folder, upload a file, or create an Office file such as a Word document. The *Scan* option can be used to take a photo from your phone and have it directly uploaded to your OneDrive account.

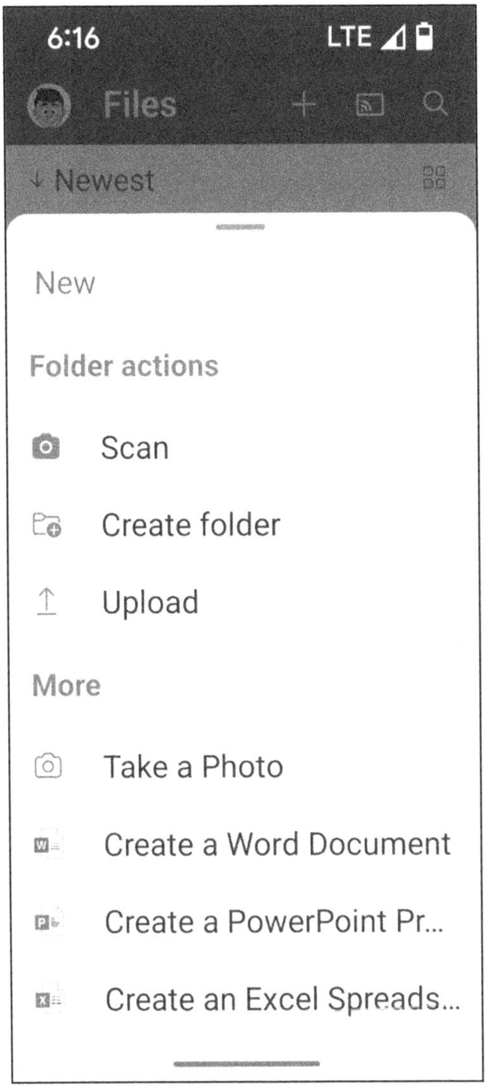

Figure 2.23

If you were to go to the *Me* section, you would be able to see details of your plan such as how much space you have used. You can also come here to configure the settings for the app.

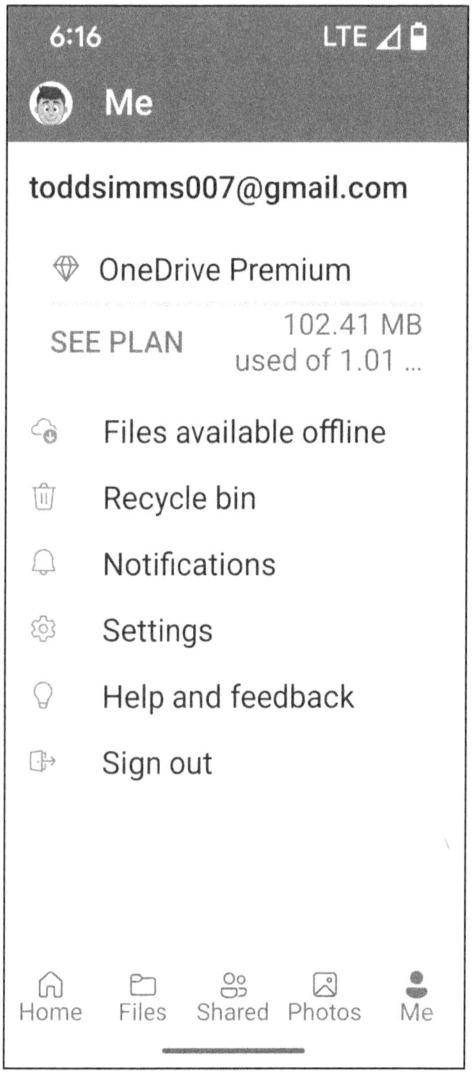
6:16
LTE
Me
toddsimms007@gmail.com
OneDrive Premium
SEE PLAN
102.41 MB
used of 1.01 ...
Files available offline
Recycle bin
Notifications
Settings
Help and feedback
Sign out
Home
Files
Shared
Photos
Me

Figure 2.24

Chapter 3 – Managing Files and Folders

If you end up being a serious OneDrive user, you are going to need to know how to manage your files and folders so you can do things such as edit, share, copy, move and delete them as needed.

Copying & Moving Files & Folders to Other Folders

If you have a file or folder in one directory but need to either make a copy of it or move it to another folder, it is very easy to do. Once you select the file or folder, you will see some icons appear at the top of the page where you can then choose *Move to* or *Copy to*. Figure 3.1 shows the choices you have when selecting a folder while Figure 3.2 shows the choices you have when selecting a file with the main difference being that you have an *Open* option when choosing a file.

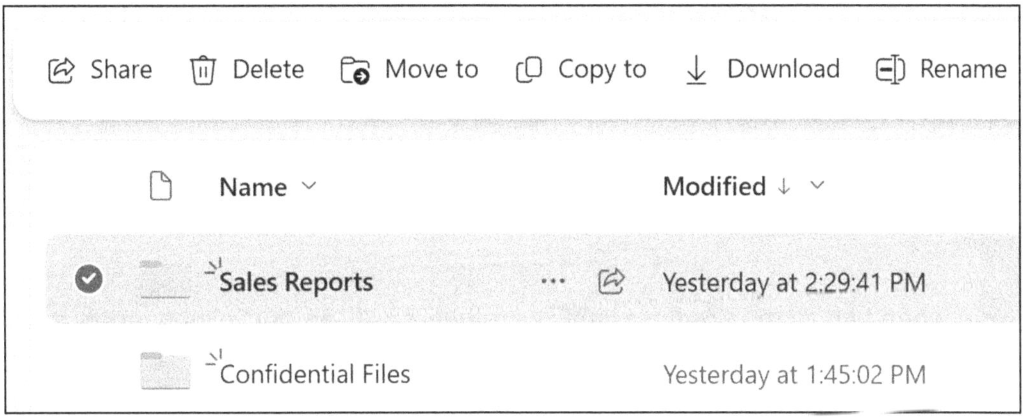

Figure 3.1

Figure 3.2

When you select multiple items, you will most likely see fewer options since OneDrive can't do things such as rename multiple files or folders at once.

I will now move my Sales Reports folder to my Confidential Files folder by selecting the Sales Report folder, clicking on the *Move to* button, and then selecting the Confidential Files folder.

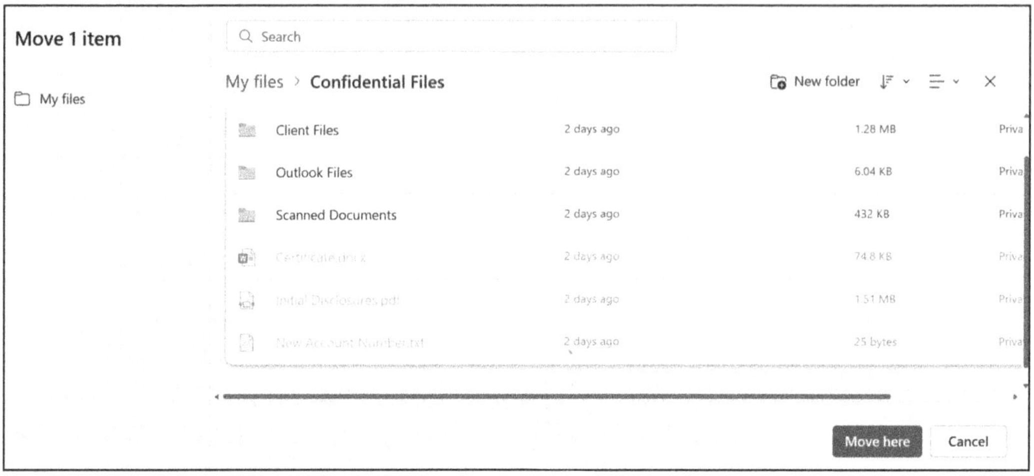

Figure 3.3

After I click the *Move here* button, the folder will be moved to its new location, and I will see a message pop up telling me that it has been moved.

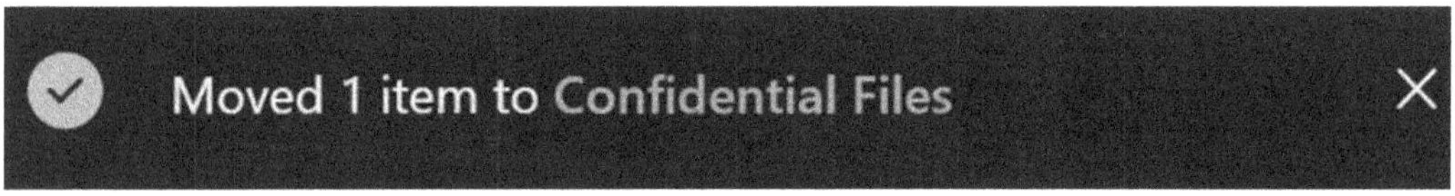

Figure 3.4

Now when I go to my Confidential Files folder, I will see my Sales Reports folder there and it will no longer be under the My files section.

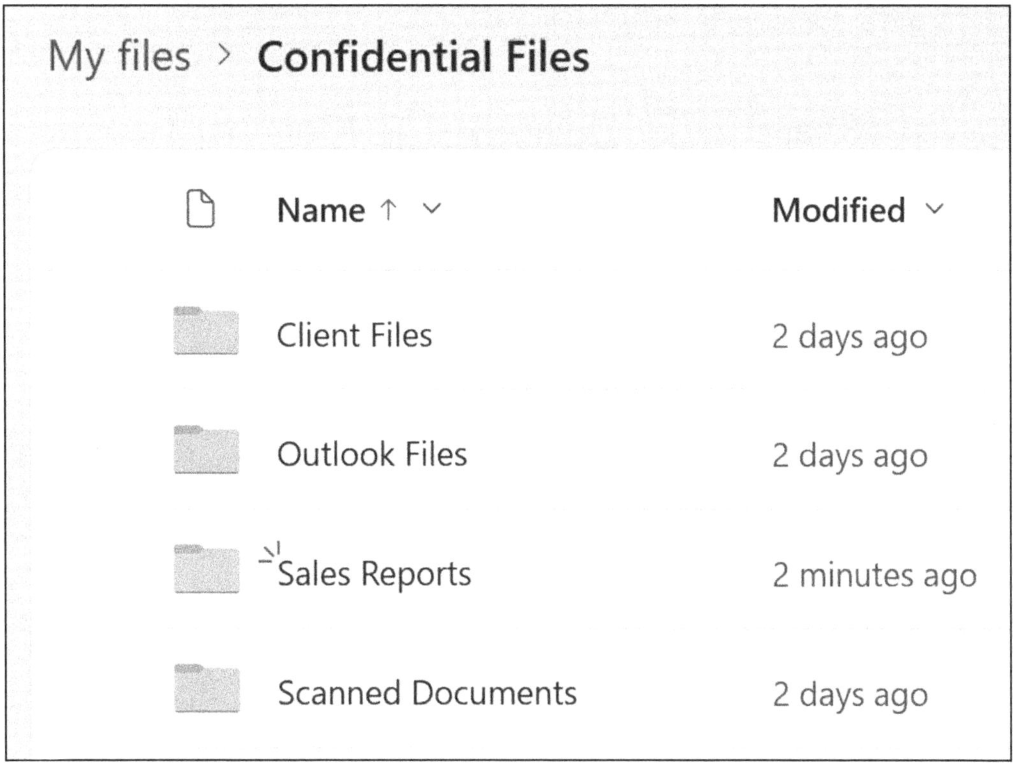

Figure 3.5

The process to copy a file or folder works the same way except once you copy the file or folder, you will still have the original in the original folder along with the copy in the new location.

Deleting Files & Restoring Items from the Trash

When it comes to removing unwanted files and folders from OneDrive, you can delete them as needed just like you can files and folders on your PC.

When you select a file or folder, you will have a *Delete* option that appears in the toolbar above your file list.

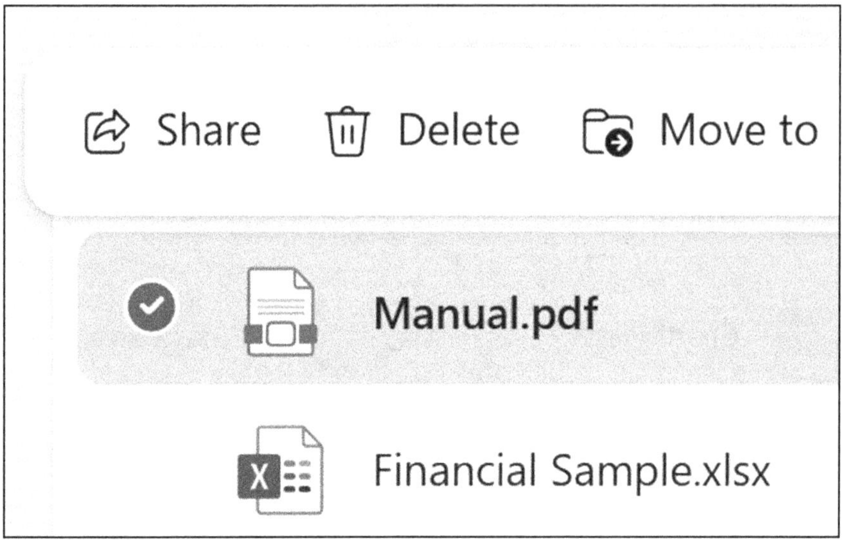

Figure 3.6

When you click on this button, you will be asked to confirm that you want to delete the file or folder.

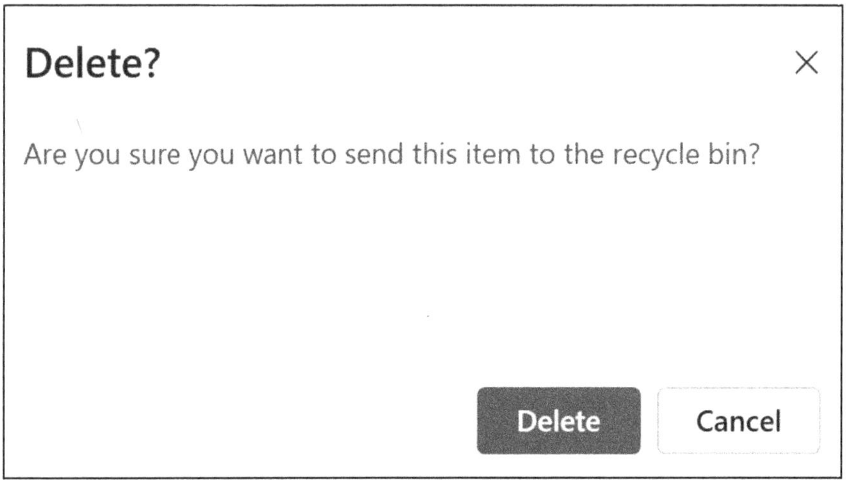

Figure 3.7

You will then be shown a popup message that tells you how many items have been deleted.

Figure 3.8

If you want to see your deleted items, you can click on the *Recycle bin* option on the left side of the page. Here you can sort by name, original location, date deleted, size and so on.

Deleted items will stay in the Recycle bin for 30 days before they are permanently deleted. There is a chance they will stay longer but you should assume they will be automatically deleted at some point.

Once you are in the Recycle bin, you have the option to empty the recycle bin which will permanently delete all the files and folders here or restore all the items here to their original location. You also have an option to see items deleted from the Personal Vault which will be discussed later in this chapter.

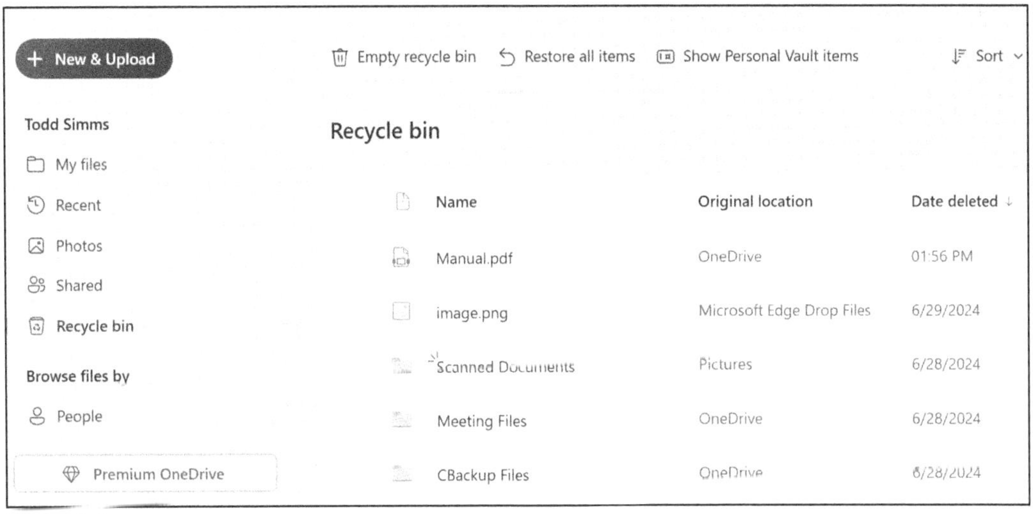

Figure 3.9

When you select a file or folder in the Recycle bin, you will then have the option to delete it permanently or restore it back to its original location.

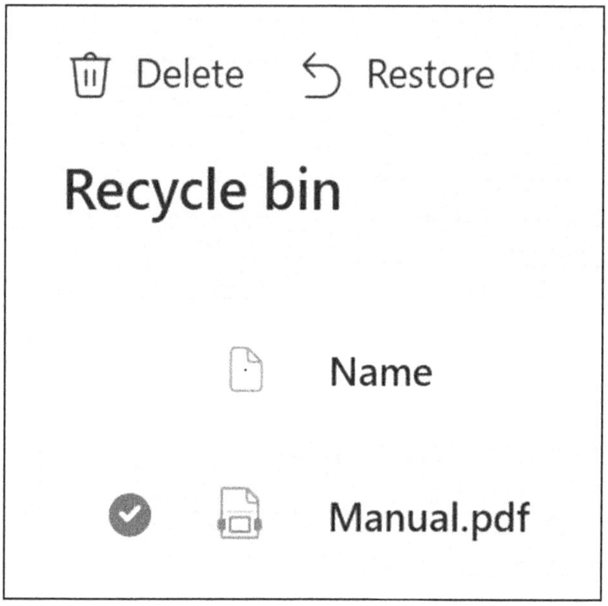

Figure 3.10

Downloading Files to Your Computer
If you prefer to work on your files locally on your computer rather than in the cloud, you can easily download them to your PC, make changes and then upload them again.

When downloading a single file, you will be prompted as to where you want to save the file. You can also change the name of the file during the save process.

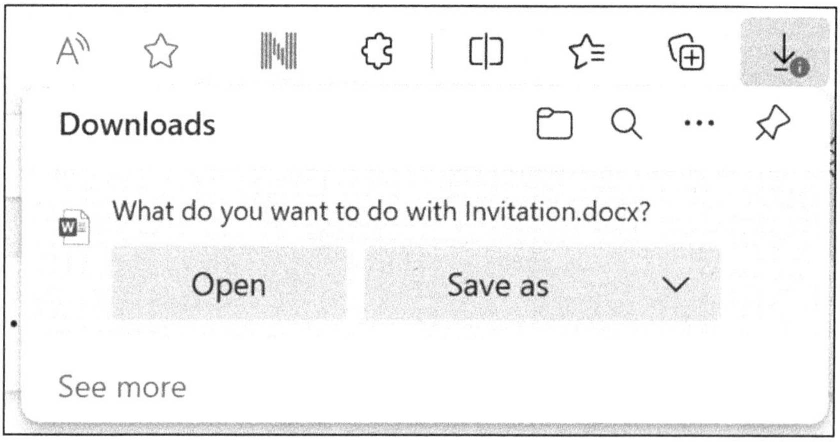

Figure 3.11

If you select multiple files, OneDrive will create a zip file containing those files that you can download and then extract once you have the zip file on your PC.

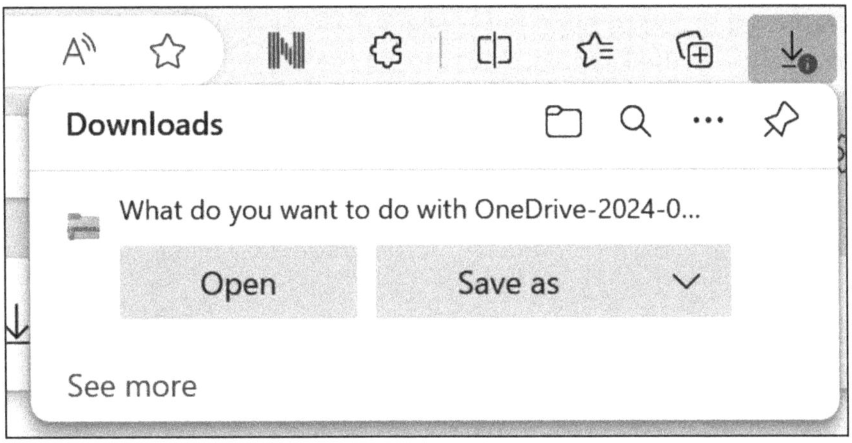

Figure 3.12

When you download a folder, OneDrive will create a zip file using the name of the folder that you can then unzip once you have the file downloaded.

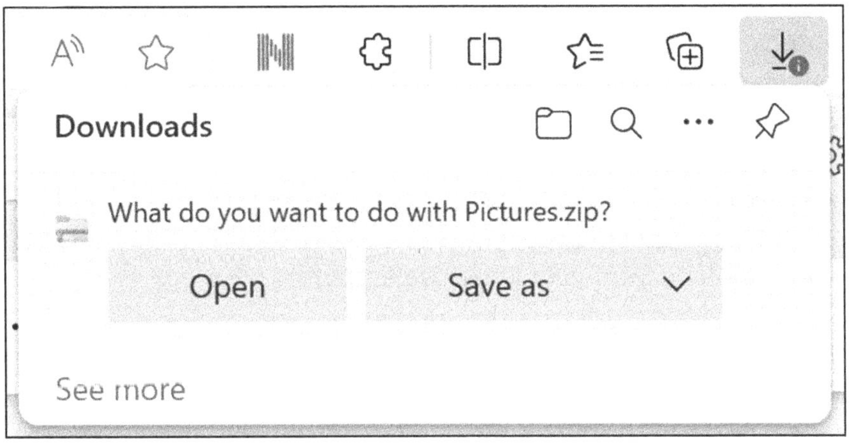

Figure 3.13

Now let's say you have downloaded a file to your computer, made some changes to it and then tried to upload it back to the same location in OneDrive. When doing this, you will see a message telling you that there is already a file with that name in that folder in your OneDrive account.

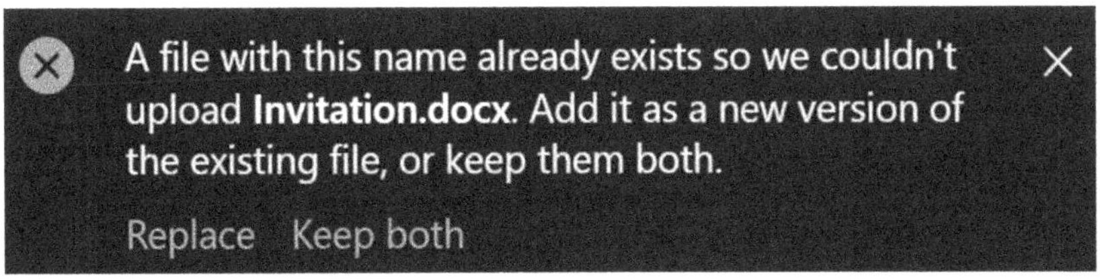

Figure 3.14

You can then replace the file to have the uploaded file be the current and only version or you can click on the *Keep both* option to have the file uploaded without affecting the copy that is already in your drive. When you do this, the new file will be renamed with a 1 after it so you can tell them apart (Figure 3.15).

Figure 3.15

This is one reason you may want to work on your OneDrive files from the cloud rather than downloading a copy of them first. One way to work on your online files from your computer is by using the OneDrive client, which will be discussed later in this chapter.

Opening & Editing Files Within Your Browser

If you have ever used an online app such as Google Docs to create and edit documents, you may be interested to know that you can do the same thing with certain types of files directly from your OneDrive account.

Let's say you had a Microsoft Word document stored in your account, if you were to select the file, you would see an option that says *Open*. This is because Word documents are a supported file type for online viewing and editing.

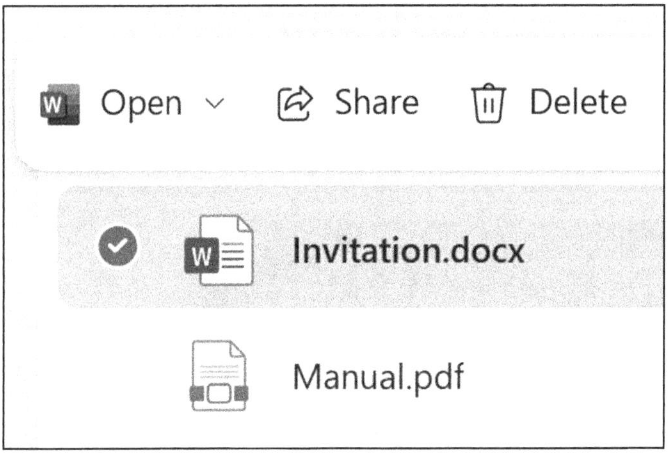

Figure 3.16

Figure 3.17 shows my Word document open within my web browser where I can then work on it and any changes will instantly be saved to my OneDrive account.

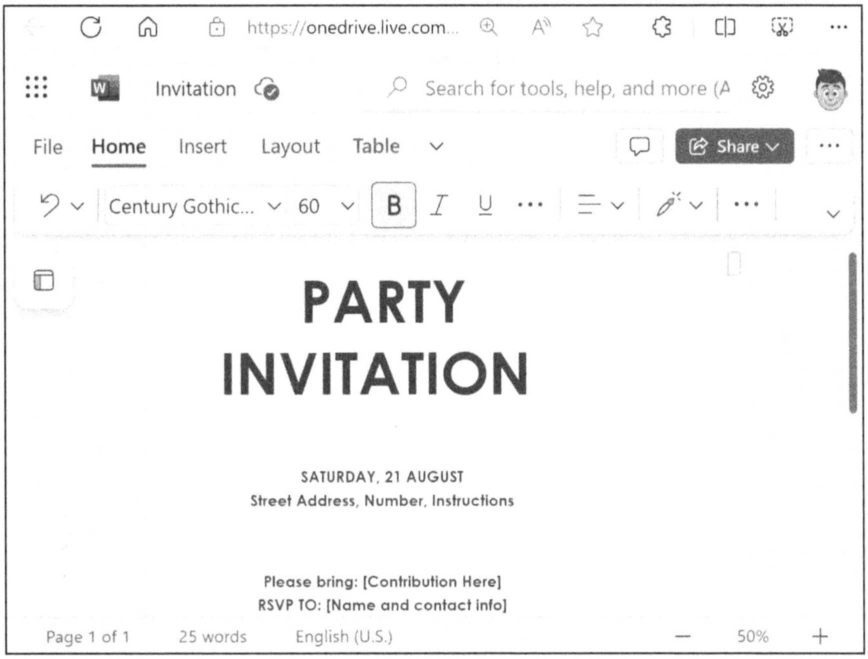

Figure 3.17

If I were to select a PDF file, you can see that I do not have an option to open it.

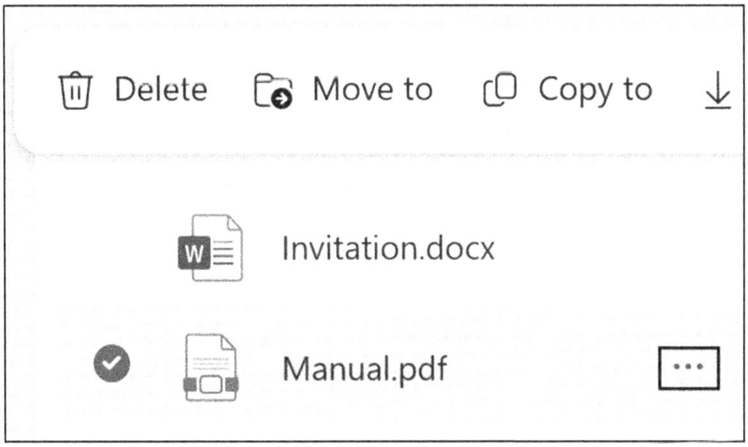

Figure 3.18

But if I were to click the ellipsis (...) next to the file name, I would have an option to preview the file within my web browser.

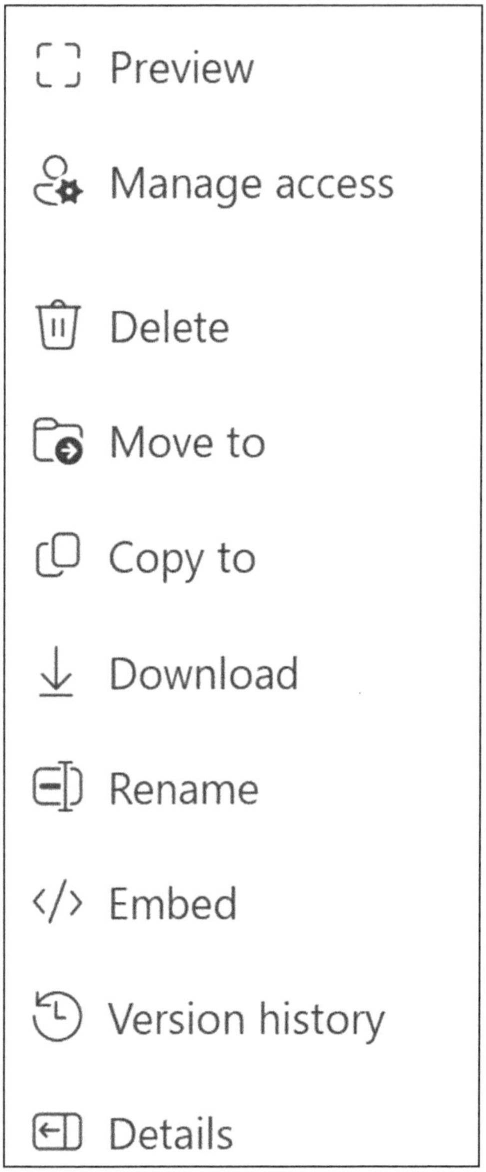

Figure 3.19

Figure 3.20 shows the PDF file open in my browser, but I do not have any way to edit the file itself. Ironically, I can click on the *Open* button to open the PDF file in Word.

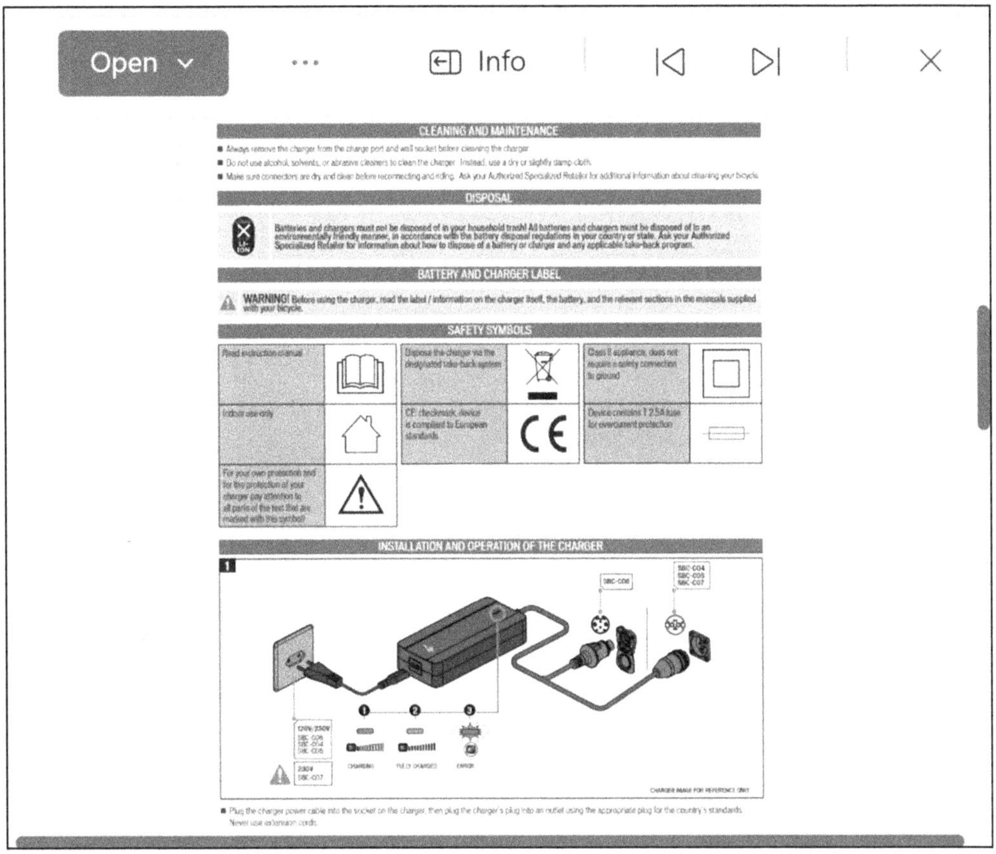

Figure 3.20

But if I were to try and edit the PDF file in Word, I would be notified that it is read-only and given an option to convert the file to a Word document. I can then click on the *Convert and Edit* button to have the PDF converted to a Word document so I can edit it as needed.

Figure 3.21

When you click this button, you will be notified that OneDrive will make a copy of your file and convert it so you can edit it.

Figure 3.22

Depending on what type of file you are trying to convert, you may see a message similar to Figure 3.23.

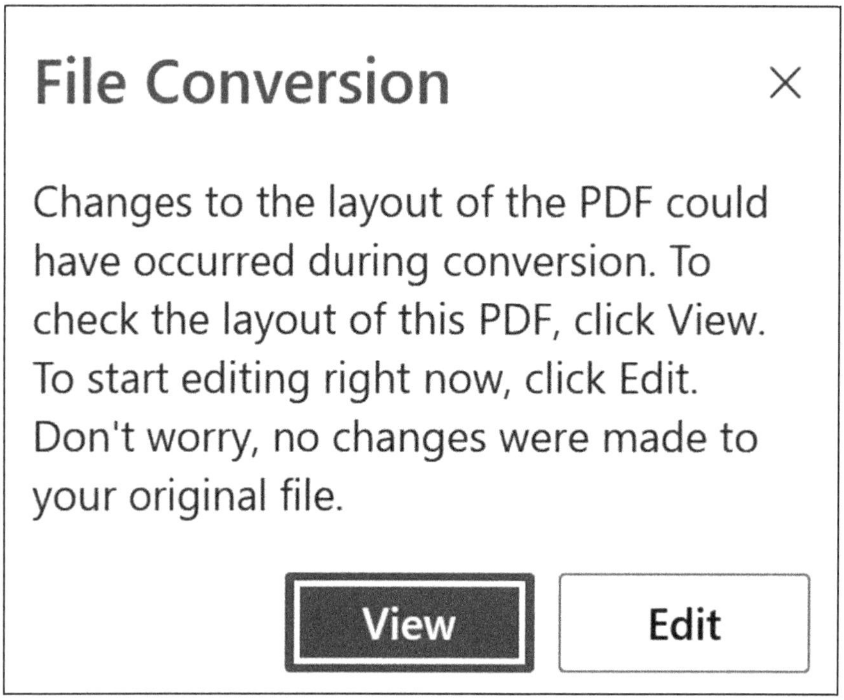

Figure 3.23

Now that the PDF file has been converted to a Word document, I can now make changes to the file and my original PDF file will not be affected.

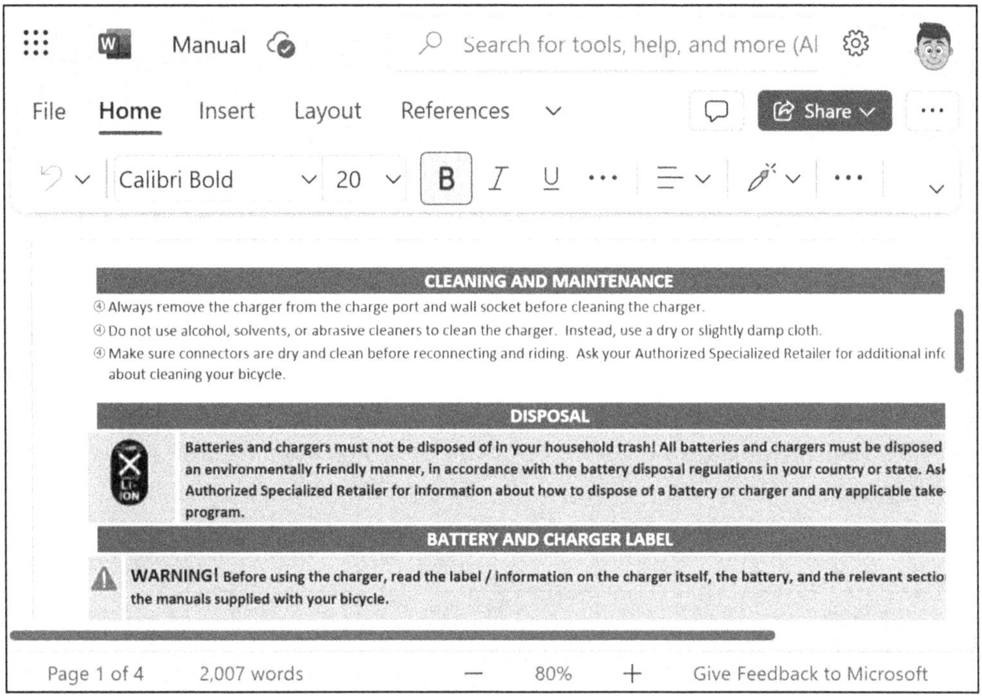

Figure 3.24

You may come across a situation where OneDrive cannot open or preview a file that you have stored in your drive. When this happens, you will need to download the file to open it on your computer assuming you have a program that can do so installed on your computer.

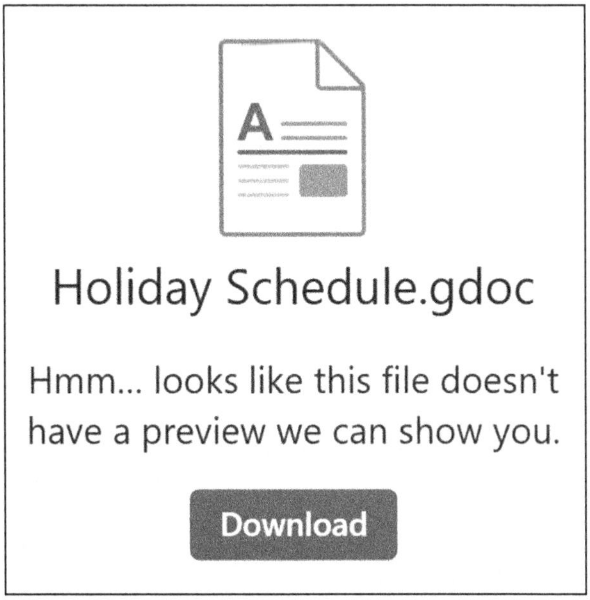

Figure 3.25

File and Folder Right Click Options

You may be used to right clicking on your files and folders while browsing them on your computer to get additional options such as cut, copy, paste, rename and so on. OneDrive has similar options you can take advantage of when right clicking on your files and folders.

Figure 3.26 shows the options you will see when right clicking on a folder. Most of these choices should be self-explanatory. The *Share* and *Manage access* choices are used for collaboration purposes and will be discussed in Chapter 5. The *Create album from folder* option is used to create a photo album from any pictures in that folder. I will be showing an example of this later in this chapter. The *Details* option is used to show various details about your folder which I will be discussing later in this chapter.

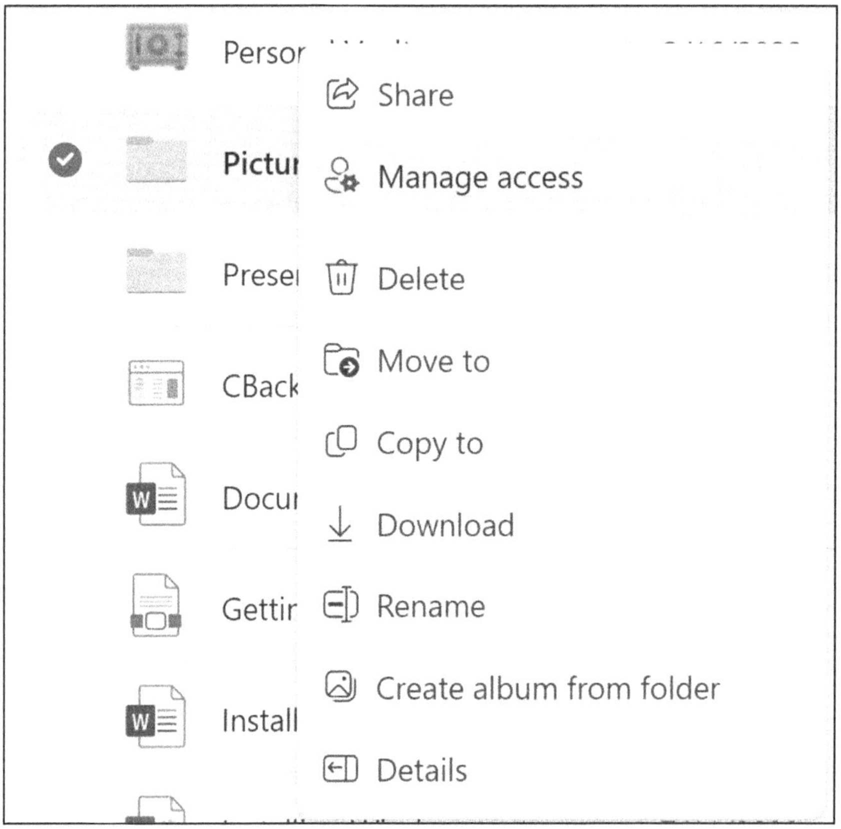

Figure 3.26

When you right click on a file, you will have a few more options as shown in Figure 3.27. The only ones that might not be self-explanatory are the *Embed* and *Version history* options.

The embed option is used to generate code that can be used to embed a folder on a web page. This way other people can access the folder right from your website. Version history is used to monitor changes to a file and will be discussed later in this chapter.

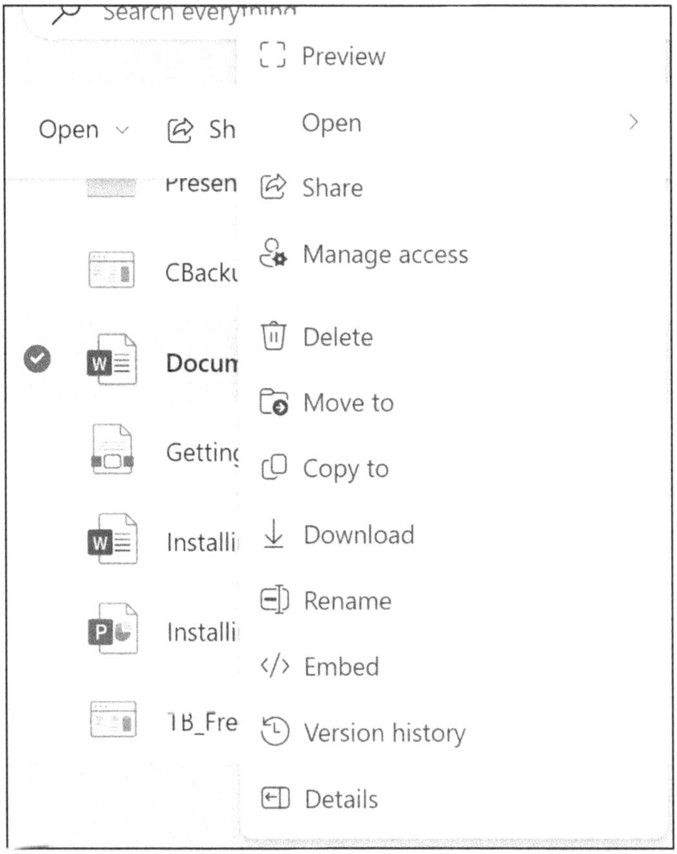

Figure 3.27

Searching for Files and Folders

Once you upload multiple files to your OneDrive account, you may find it difficult to find the files and folders you are looking for. Fortunately, OneDrive has a search feature that can help you out. The search feature is fairly basic, but you should be able to find what you need while using it.

At the top of the page, you will find the search box where you can type in a word or phrase to search your files and folders with. Figure 3.28 shows the results when I search for the word **Hawaii**. As you can see, I get results consisting of folders and files with the word Hawaii in them as well as other words along with the word Hawaii.

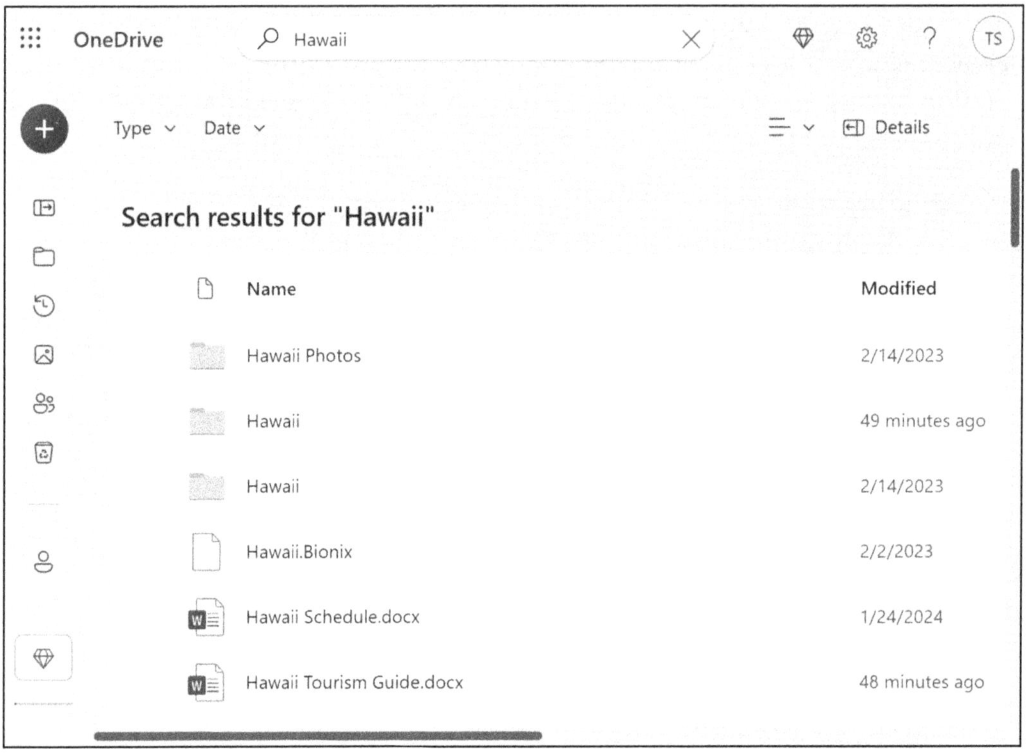

Figure 3.28

If I were to search for **Hawaii schedule**, I would only get results that contain both words.

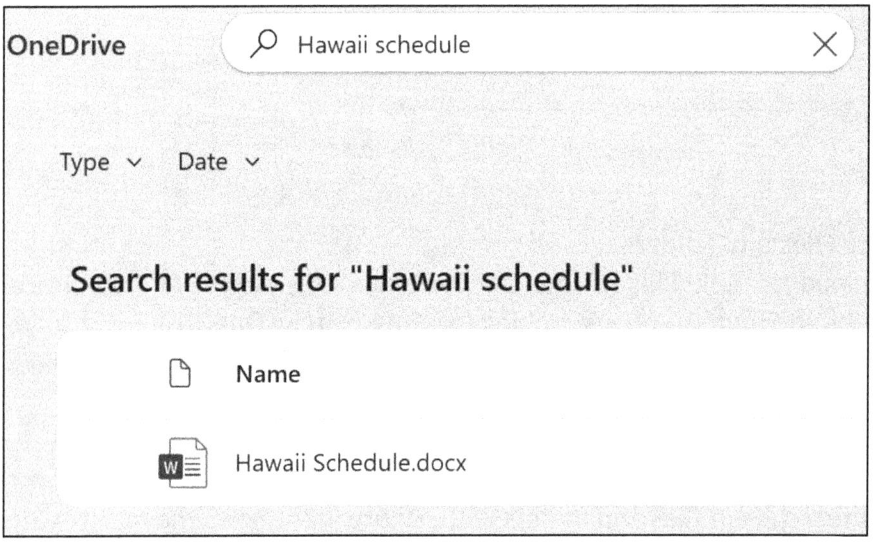

Figure 3.29

At the top of the search results, you can narrow down the results by type as seen in figure 3.30, or by date as seen in Figure 3.31.

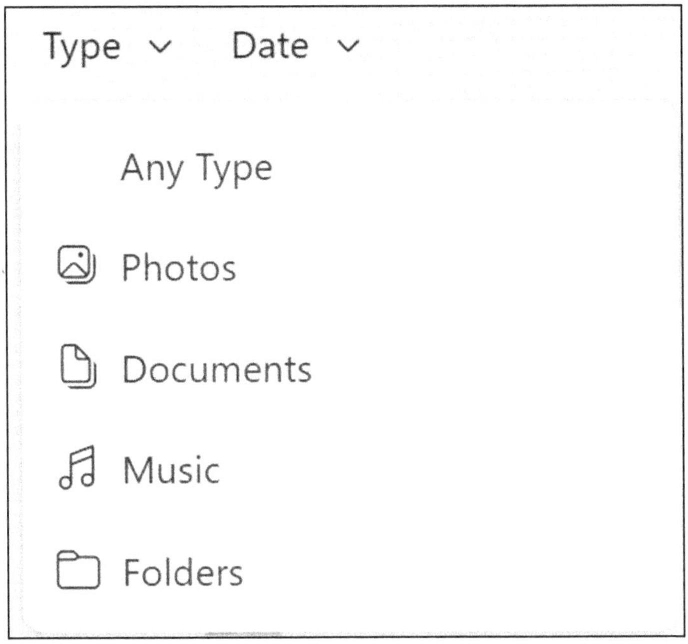

Figure 3.30

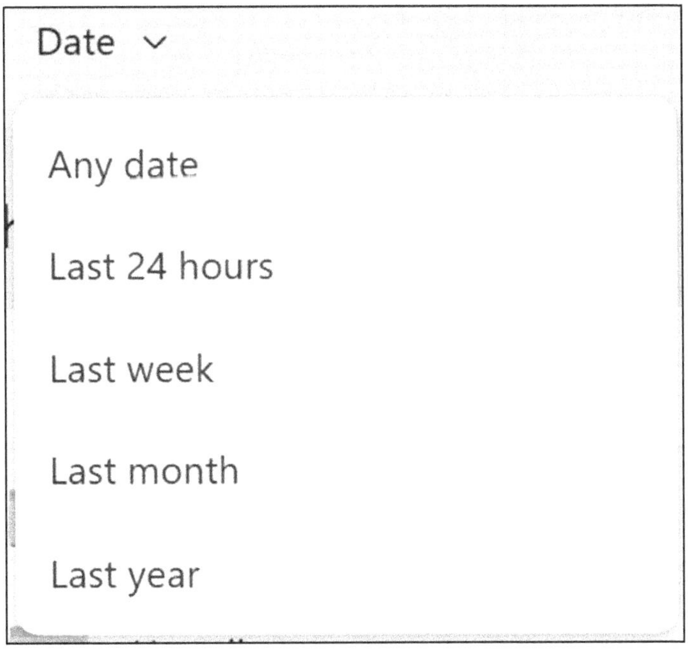

Figure 3.31

Going back to my original search for the word Hawaii, I can change the type to Photos and OneDrive will only show results that are photo files (Figure 3.32).

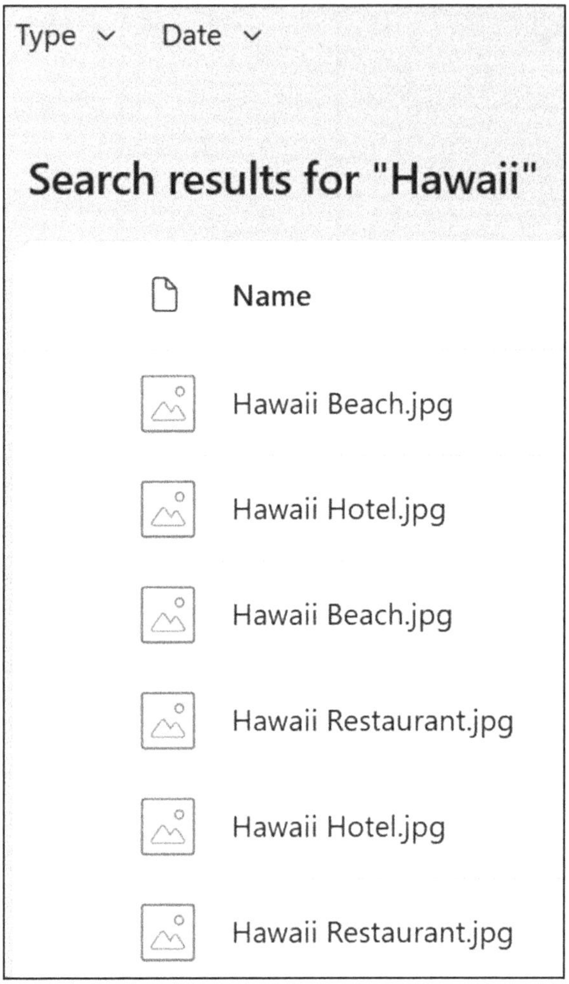

Figure 3.32

Version History

One of the best features of keeping files in the cloud is that many of these services will keep multiple versions of your files so you have a way to view or go back to older versions. Let's say you were working on a document online and made some changes that you are not happy with. Rather than try and undo the changes, you can simply revert back to an older version that was saved before these changes were made.

When you right click on a file or click on the ellipsis, you will have an option called *Version history*. If the file you are viewing the version history for is something that can be previewed online, OneDrive will show you how the current version of that file looks.

If there are other versions of the file, they will be listed to the left of the preview with their date and time. When you click on one of these older versions, you will be shown a preview of the file off to the right if it is something that can be opened in OneDrive.

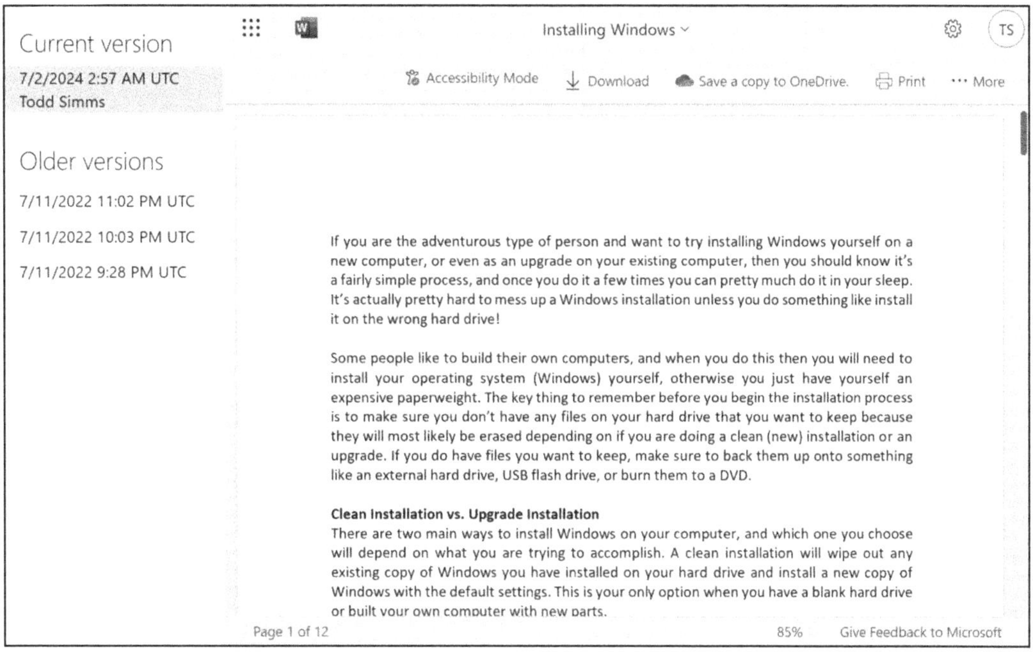

Figure 3.33

When you click on the date of an older version of the file, you will be able to either restore or download the version of that file.

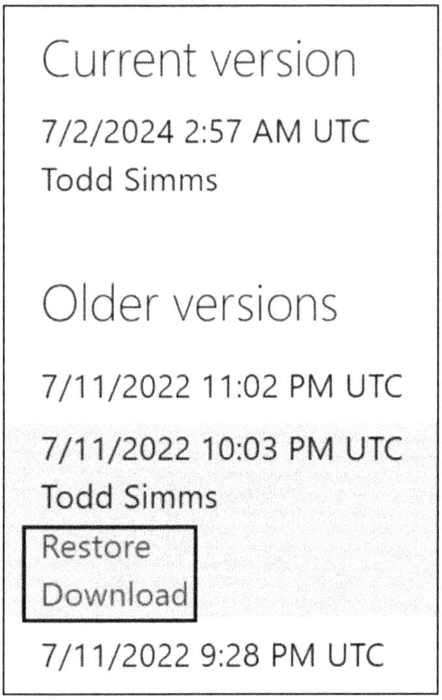

Figure 3.34

If you choose the *Restore* option, the older file will become the current version of the file and the previous current version will be listed as an older version as shown in Figure 3.35.

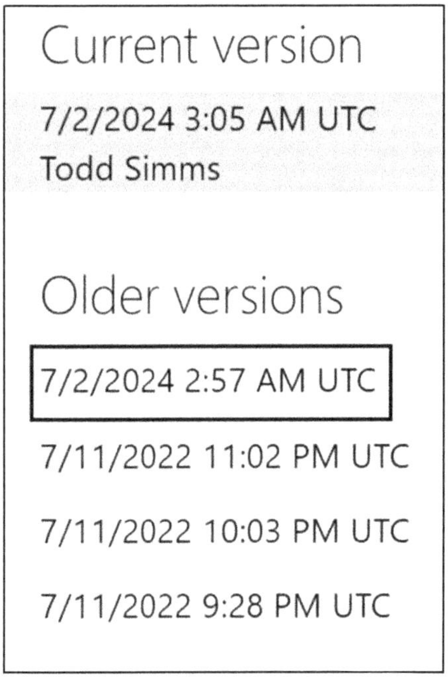

Figure 3.35

If you view the version history of a file that cannot be previewed or does not have any previous versions, you will see a screen similar to Figure 3.36. You will still have the option to open the file if possible, by clicking on the three vertical dots next to the date.

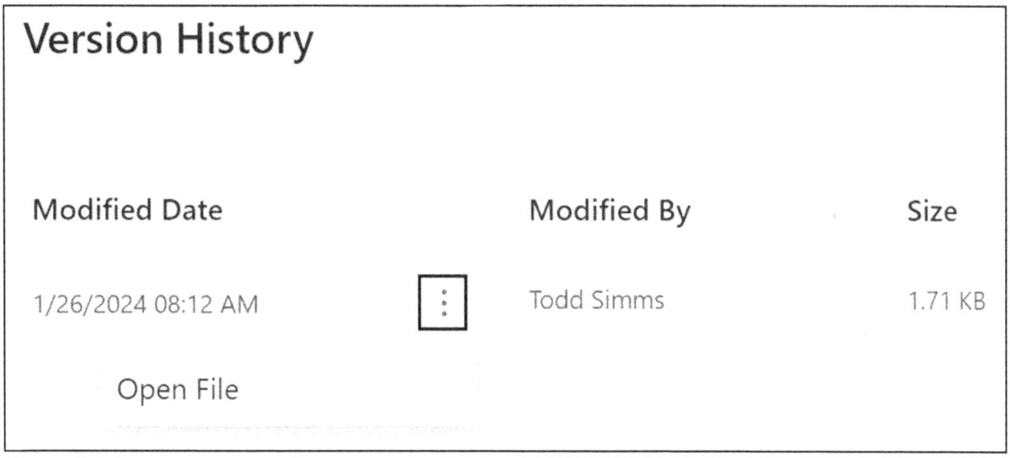

Figure 3.36

Viewing & Editing Photos

If you end up storing photos in your OneDrive account, then you may want to check out the Photos section to help you manage and view your pictures. When you click on the Photos option in the navigation section on the left, you will notice that OneDrive will display pictures from all your folders, so you do not need to navigate to different folders to see them.

Figure 3.37

If you want to change what is displayed when you click on Photos, you can do so from the dropdown menu at the upper right of the Photos page.

Figure 3.38

You can also change the view settings for the Photos section of OneDrive.

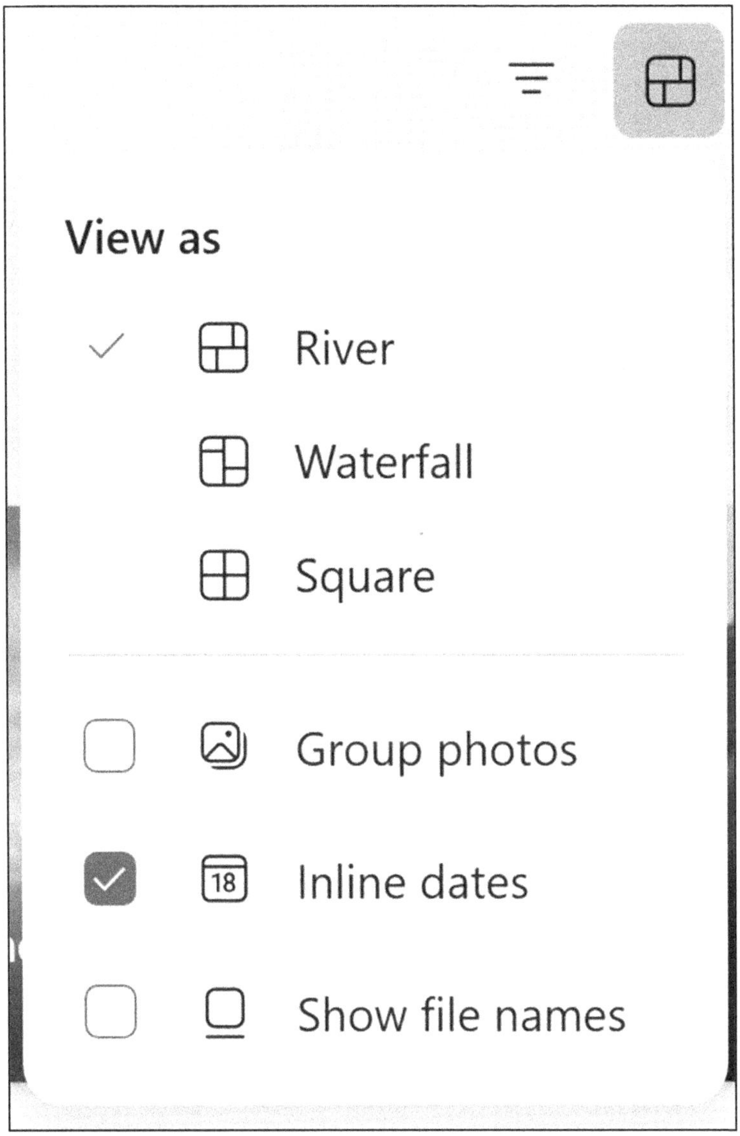

Figure 3.39

When you go to the Explore section, you will see that OneDrive tries to categorize your photos based on what it sees in the pictures themselves (known as tagging). If you have photos in folders then it will use the folder name to group your pictures, otherwise it will simply go by what it sees in the photos. You will find that many times, the way it groups the photos is not too accurate.

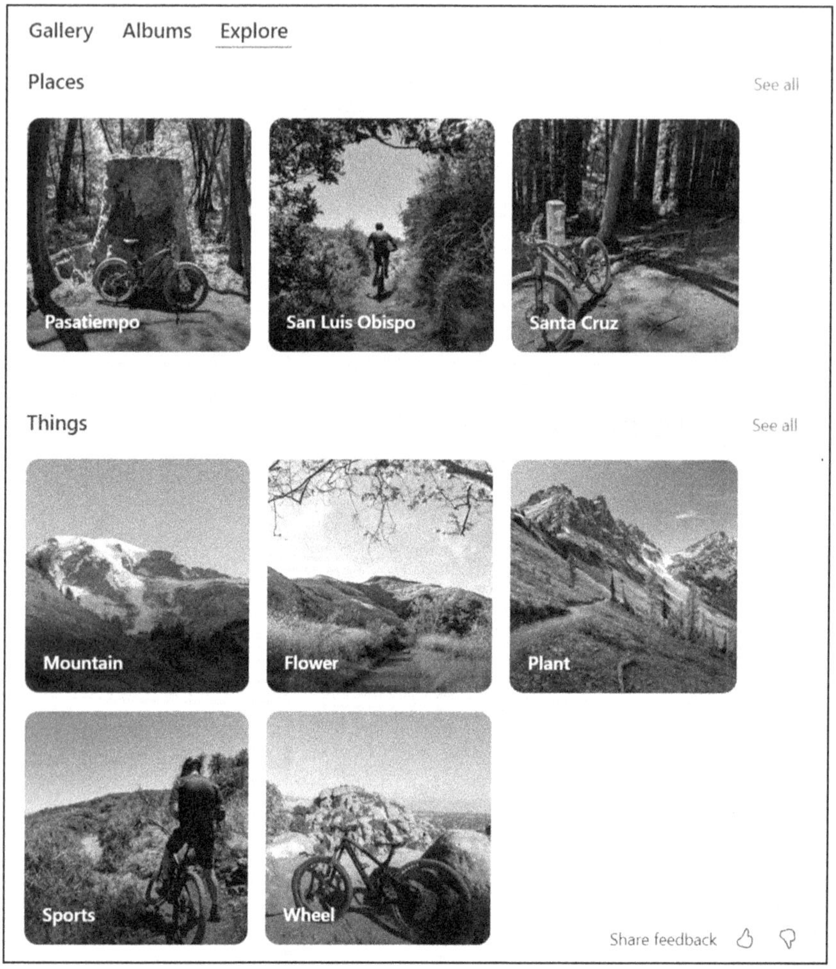

Figure 3.40

At the bottom of the Explore section, you will have some categories that you can click on to see if OneDrive happened to group your photos accurately.

Figure 3.41

The *Albums* section is where you can go to create your own photo albums. All you need to do is give your album a name and add photos from your OneDrive account. Once you have the album created, you can add more photos to it later as you add them to your OneDrive account.

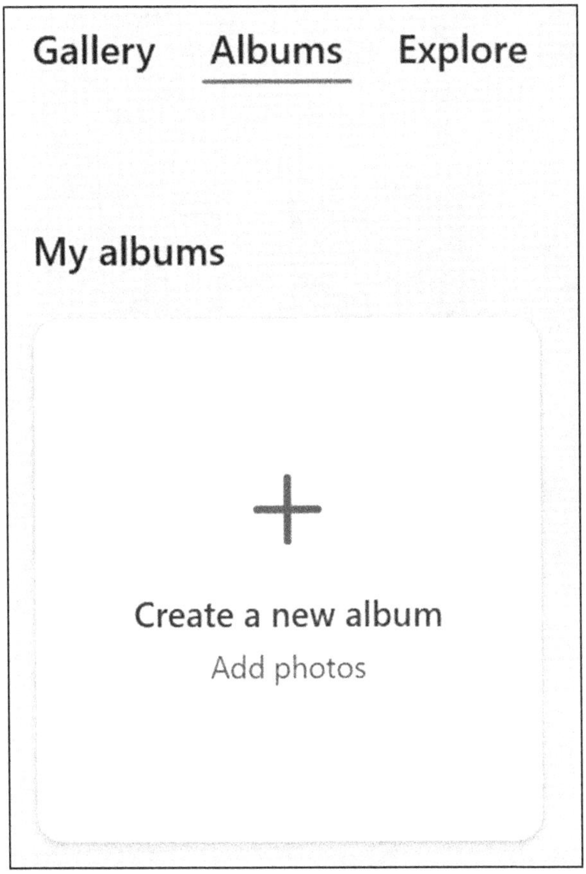

Figure 3.42

If you have a folder that contains photos, you can right click on it and choose *Create album from folder*. When you choose this option, OneDrive will take any photos contained in that folder and create a photo album from them.

Figure 3.43 shows that there are several photos in the folder as well as a Word document. OneDrive will ignore the Word document and create a photo album from the pictures themselves.

Figure 3.43

When you choose the Create album from folder option, you will see the album being created and then you will receive a message when the process is complete.

Figure 3.44

Now when you go back to the Albums section under Photos, you will see your newly created album listed with any others you might have.

Figure 3.45

When you open the album, you will see all the photos that were contained in that folder.

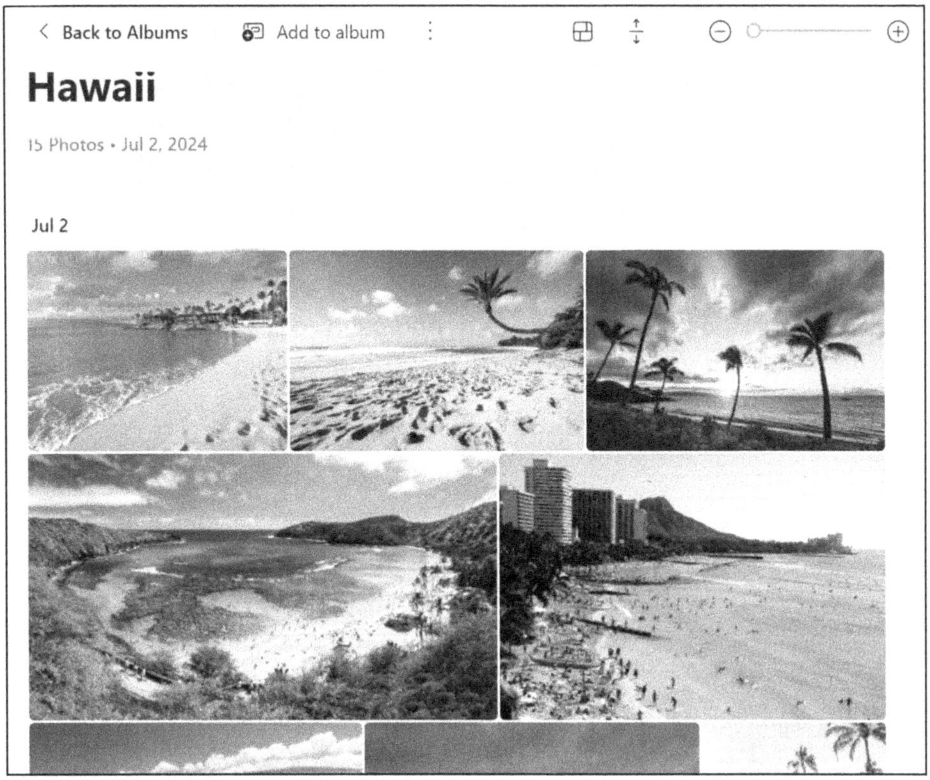

Figure 3.46

Many people like to edit their own photos and OneDrive has a basic built in photo editor that you can use to do so. When you open a photo, you will see an *Edit* button that you can click on to open the photo editor.

Figure 3.47

Once you are in edit mode, you will see various options at the top of the screen to do things such as crop the photo, change its lighting and color properties, and even apply a custom filter to your photo (Figures 3.48 through 3.50).

Figure 3.48

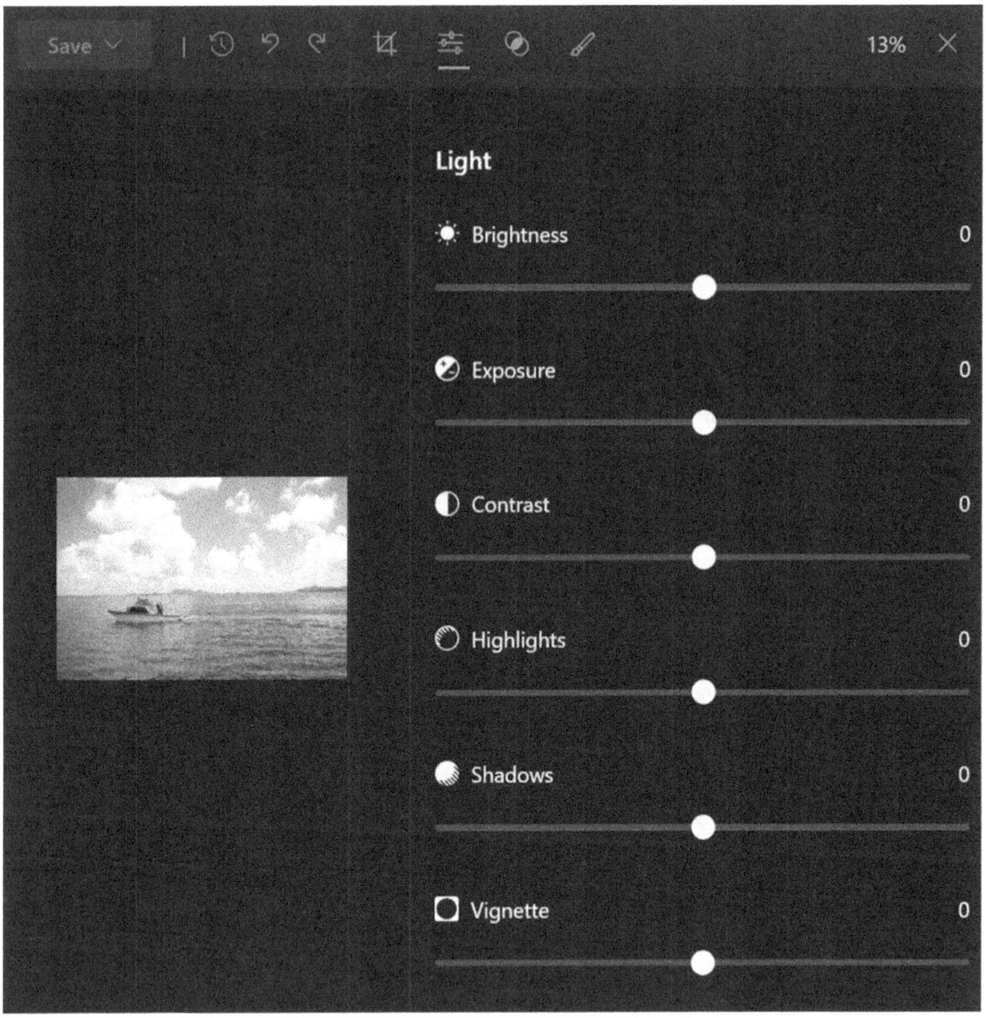
Save
13%
Light
Brightness
0
Exposure
0
Contrast
0
Highlights
0
Shadows
0
Vignette
0
Figure 3.49

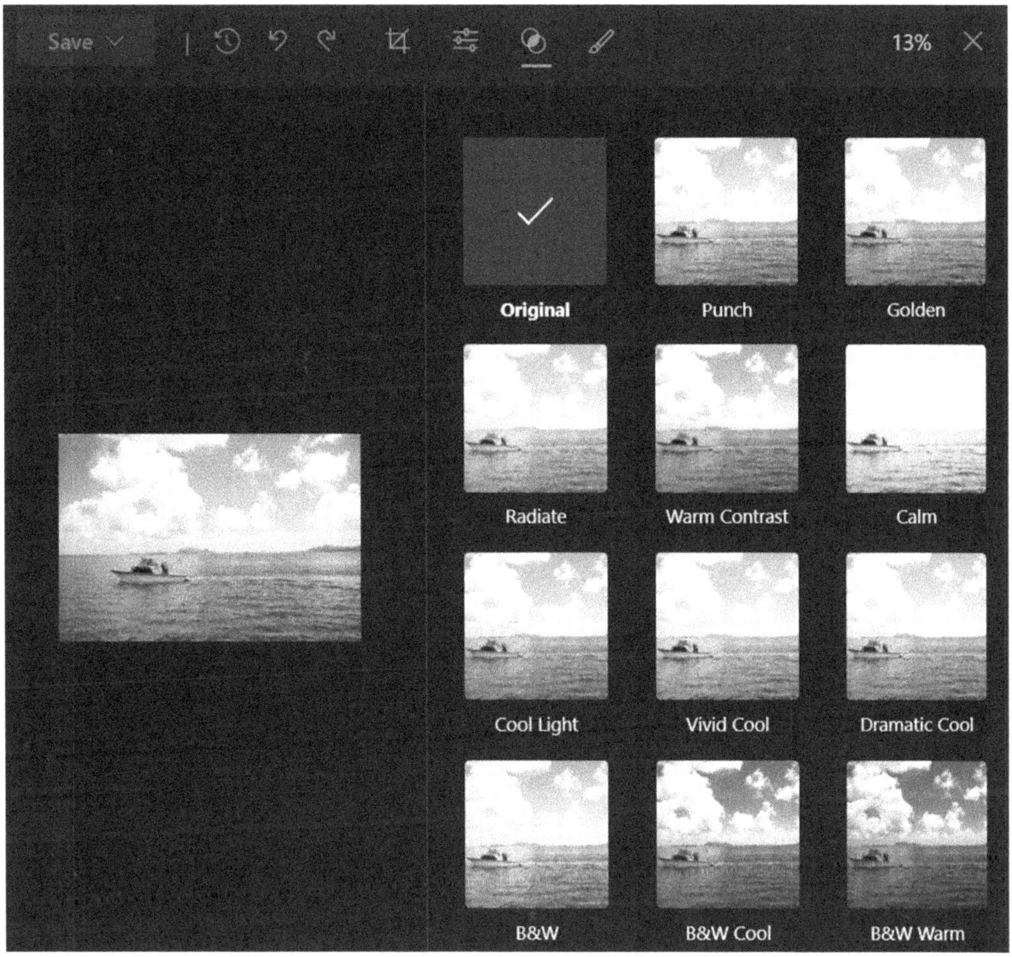

Figure 3.50

Once you make your changes, you can either save the photo and overwrite the current version, or you can choose the *save as* option to save it with a different name or in a different folder so you will still have the original copy as is. There are also undo and redo buttons at the top of the window like you see in other apps such as Microsoft Word.

Details Pane

The Details pane is used to show specific information about a file or folder. Once you select one of your files or folders, you can click on the *Details* button to open the Details pane.

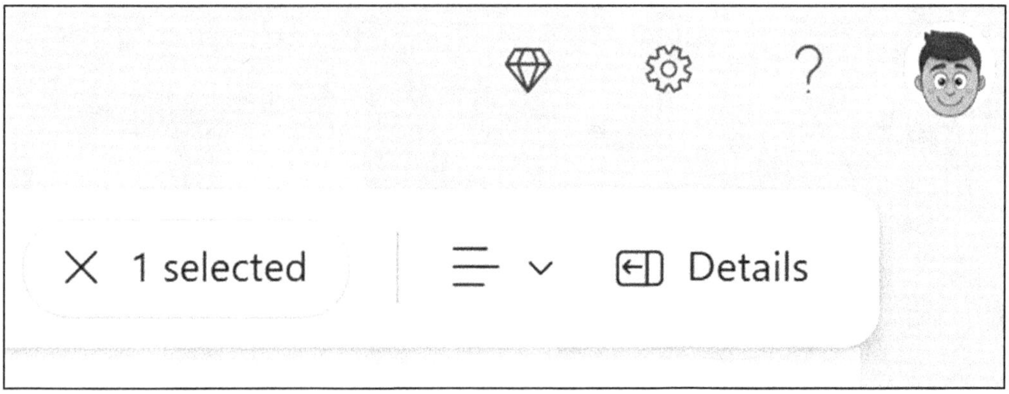

Figure 3.51

Figure 3.52 shows how the Details pane looks when a folder is selected. As you can see, it will show a preview of the contents (if it can) and then show any sharing information as well as any comments added by other users.

If you were to click on *More details*, you would see additional information such as its creation date, when it was modified, its path, and its size.

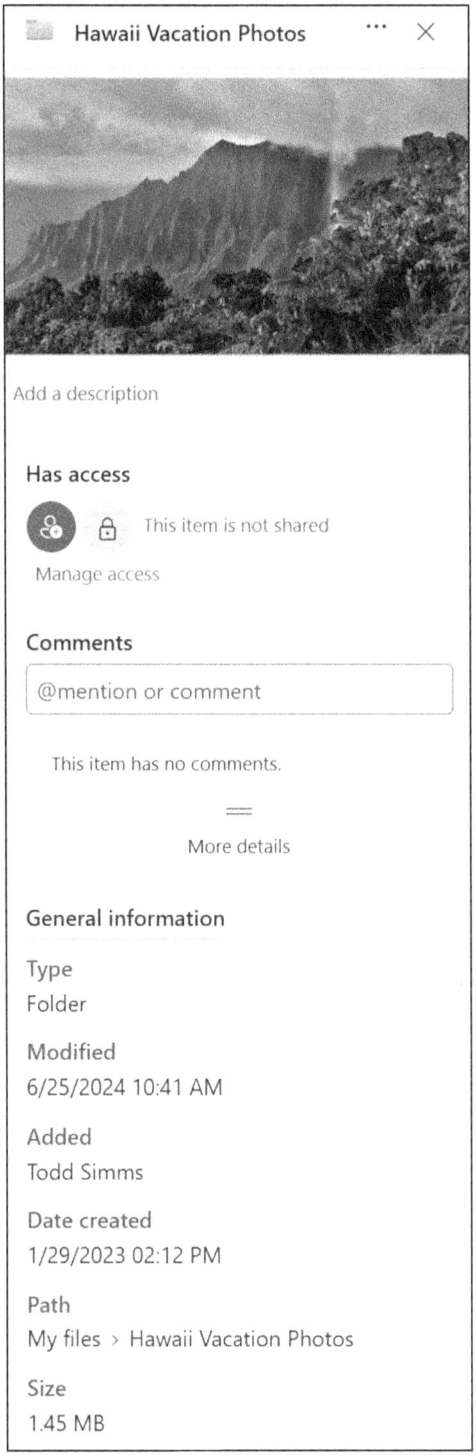
Hawaii Vacation Photos
Add a description
Has access
This item is not shared
Manage access
Comments
@mention or comment
This item has no comments.
More details
General information
Type
Folder
Modified
6/25/2024 10:41 AM
Added
Todd Simms
Date created
1/29/2023 02:12 PM
Path
My files › Hawaii Vacation Photos
Size
1.45 MB
Figure 3.52

Figure 3.53 shows the Details pane when a file is selected. As you can see, it will show a preview of the file if applicable as well as the same sharing information as you saw for the folder details. It will show you some version history for the file as well. The *More details* section will show you the same type of information you saw for the folder example.

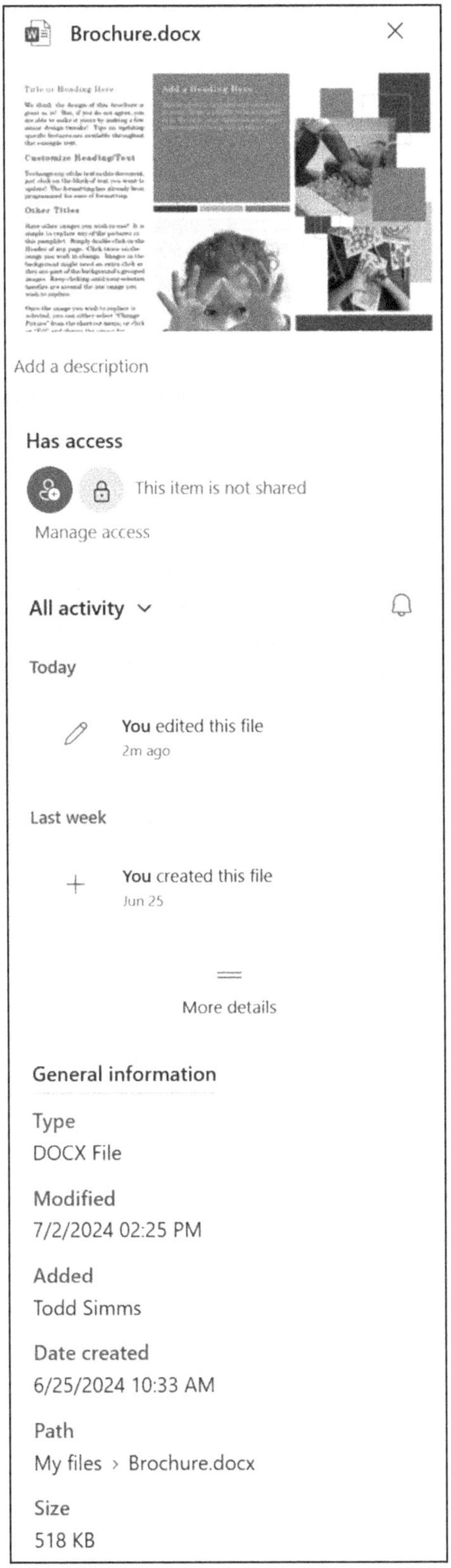
Brochure.docx
Add a description
Has access
This item is not shared
Manage access
All activity
Today
You edited this file
2m ago
Last week
You created this file
Jun 25
More details
General information
Type
DOCX File
Modified
7/2/2024 02:25 PM
Added
Todd Simms
Date created
6/25/2024 10:33 AM
Path
My files › Brochure.docx
Size
518 KB

Figure 3.53

When I get into the discussion on sharing and collaboration, you will see how the Details pane can really come in handy.

Personal Vault

The OneDrive Personal Vault is a secure area within OneDrive designed to store and protect sensitive and important files. It provides an extra layer of security for your files, ensuring they are better protected from unauthorized access. Here are the key features and uses of the Personal Vault:

- **Two-Step Verification**: To access the Personal Vault, you need to go through a two-step verification process, such as a fingerprint, face recognition, PIN, or a code sent via email or SMS.

- **Automatic Locking**: The Personal Vault automatically locks after a period of inactivity. This means even if you forget to lock it, the files inside remain protected.

- **Encryption**: Files stored in the Personal Vault are encrypted, providing an additional layer of security both in transit and at rest.

- **Secure Scanning and Upload**: You can scan documents directly into the Personal Vault using the OneDrive mobile app.

- **Available Across Other Devices**: The Personal Vault can be accessed from various devices, such as PCs, smartphones, and tablets.

When you go to the My files section in OneDrive, you will see your Personal Vault there and it will have an icon that looks like a safe.

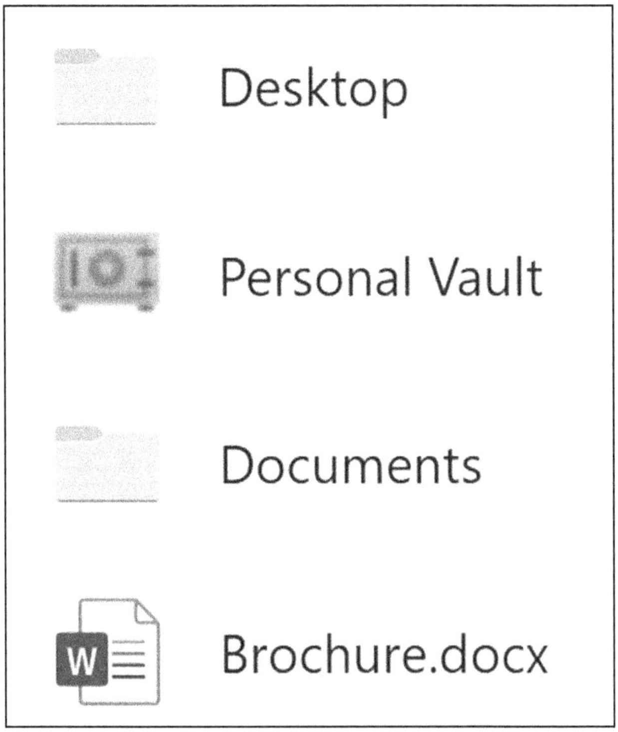

Figure 3.54

When you try to open your Personal Vault, you will receive a popup message telling you that OneDrive will send a code to the email address associated with your account. Then you will need to type in that code to proceed.

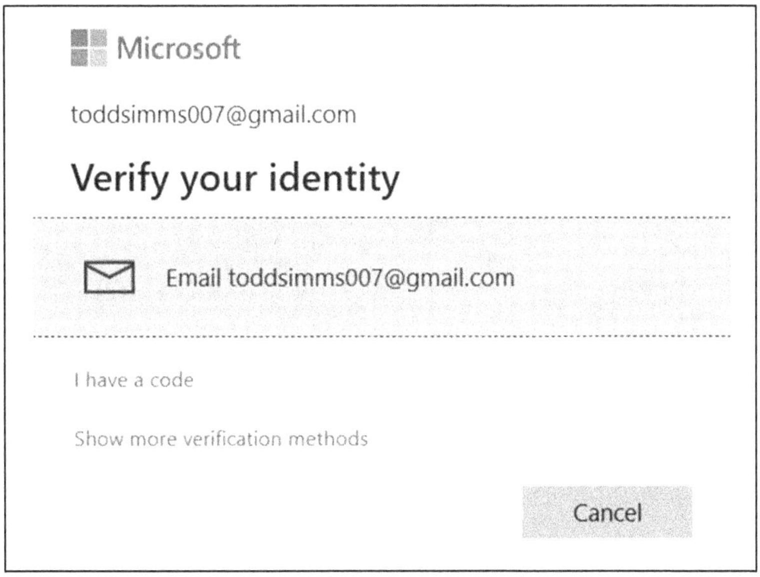

Figure 3.55

After you enter the code, you will see that your Personal Vault is now unlocked.

Figure 3.56

Once you are in your Personal Vault, you can add and remove files and folders as well as open any files stored in the vault.

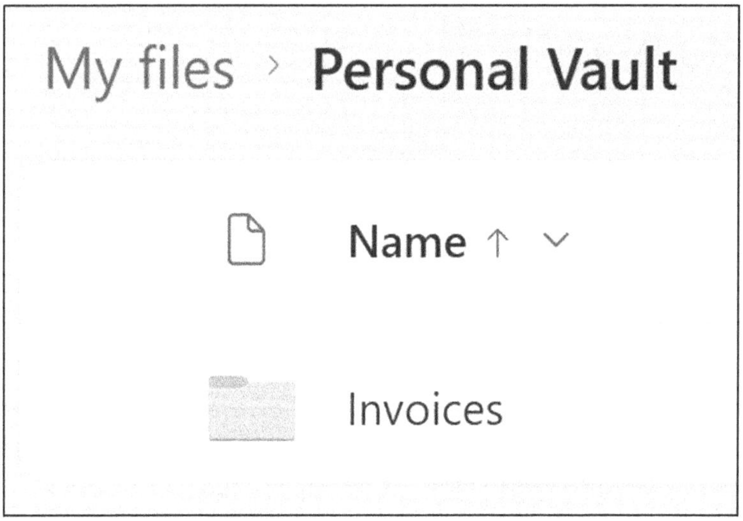

Figure 3.57

If you are using the free version of OneDrive, you are only able to store three files within your Personal Vault. If you try to add another file, you will receive a message similar to the one shown in Figure 3.58.

Figure 3.58

In order to save more files to your Personal Vault, you will need a Microsoft 365 account. If you have a paid Office 365 account, then you will not have this restriction on your Personal Vault.

Chapter 4 – Syncing Files and Folders With Your PC

If you decide that you want to be a serious OneDrive user and want to use it for things such as file backup and synchronization, you may want to consider installing the OneDrive desktop client app on your computer.

Installing the OneDrive Desktop Client

You can use the OneDrive desktop client to sync your files and folders between your desktop computer and your online OneDrive storage account. This will not sync everything on your computer but rather only the files and folders that you specify.

One important thing I want to mention is that when you install the OneDrive app on your computer, it will change the default folders for things such as Documents and Pictures and if you want to get things back to the way they were, it can be a bit of a chore to do so.

Figure 4.1 shows the default location for the Documents folder on this computer. *C:\Users\todds\Documents*

Figure 4.1

Once you start using the OneDrive client, the folder location will be changed to: *C:\Users\todds**OneDrive**\Documents*

Then if you stop using the OneDrive client, your documents will still be in this folder, and you will need to take some steps to get things back to their defaults. We have an article and video showing how to do so on our website. https://onlinecomputertips.com/support-categories/windows/change-windows-folder-locations-from-onedrive/

If you are running Windows 11 on your computer, you should already have the OneDrive client installed and it might even be running, and you may not even know it. If not, you can go to the OneDrive website, click on the gear icon, and choose *Get the OneDrive app*.

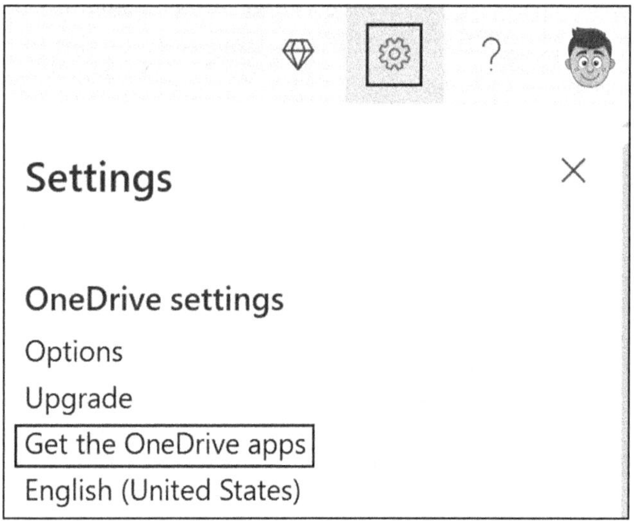

Figure 4.2

Then you will be able to download and install the OneDrive client, or you could click on *Start OneDrive* if it's already installed on your computer. You should also be able to find the OneDrive shortcut on your Windows Start menu.

Figure 4.3

If you are not already logged into the OneDrive app, you will need to do so using the same credentials you use for the OneDrive website.

Figure 4.4

You should then be shown the location of the OneDrive folder on your computer and will have the opportunity to change it if desired.

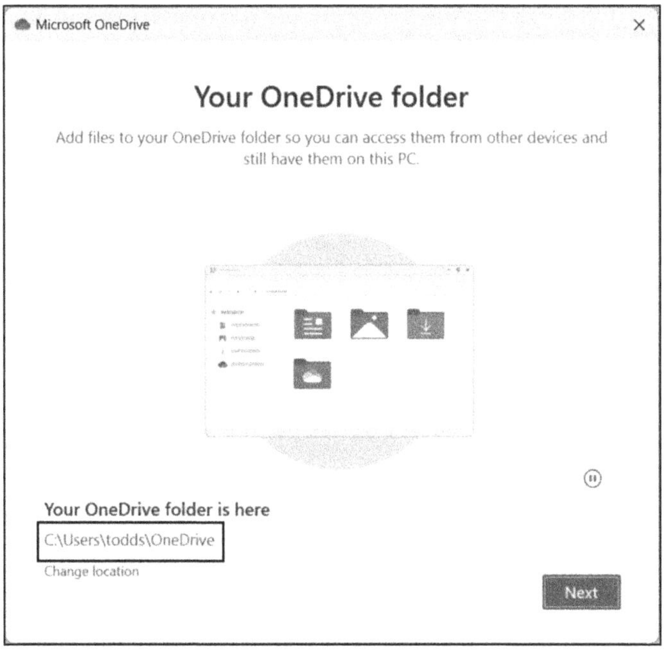

Figure 4.5

On the next screen, you will be asked which folders you want to backup\sync to your OneDrive online storage. By default, Documents, Pictures and Desktop will be selected but you can add your Music and Video folders as well as remove folders from the backup.

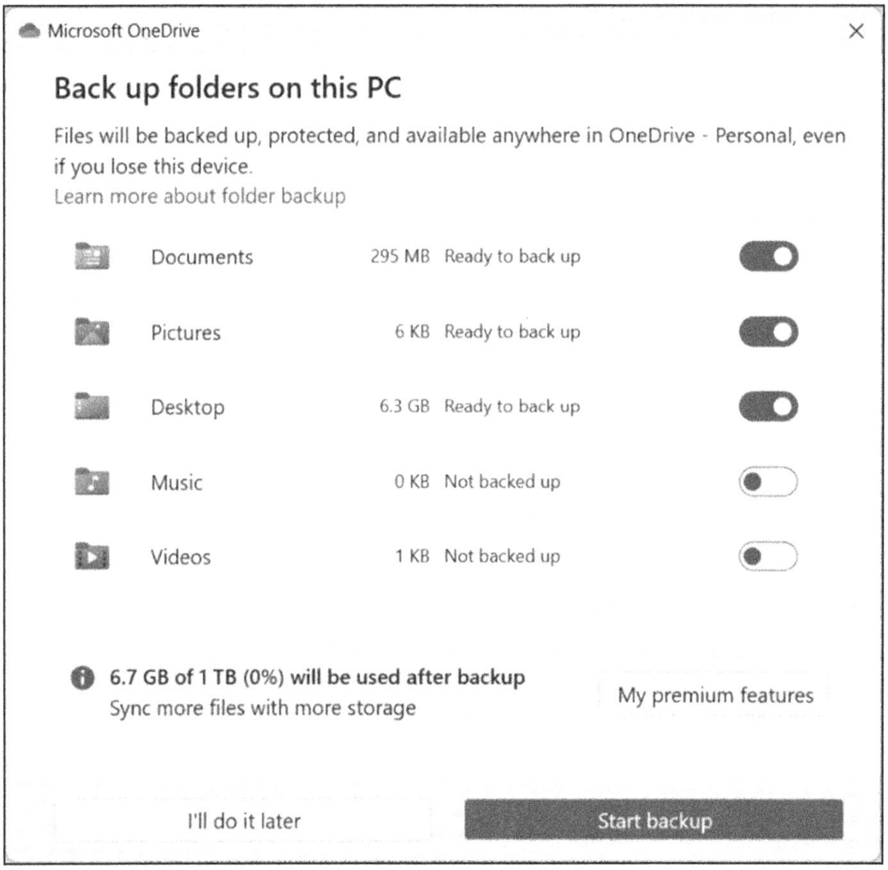

Figure 4.6

When everything is set up, you should see a message telling you that OneDrive is ready to go.

Figure 4.7

Now when you go to the newly configured OneDrive folder, you will see the same files and folders as you do when you go to the OneDrive website.

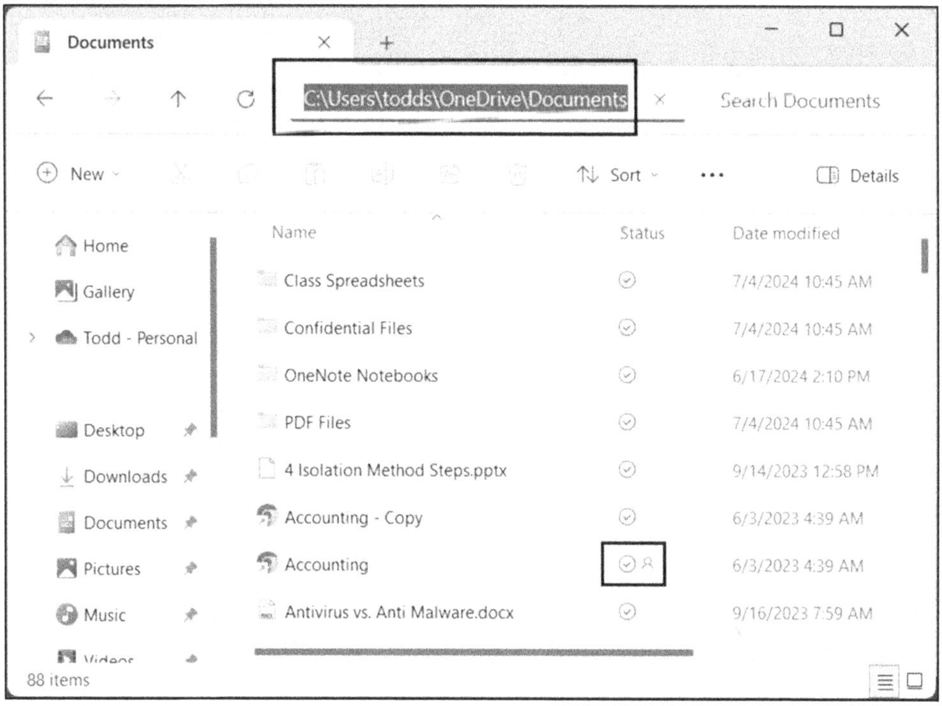

Figure 4.8

If you are using the Details view in Windows File Explorer, you will have a Status column with various icons indicating their status on your computer. Here is what each of them means.

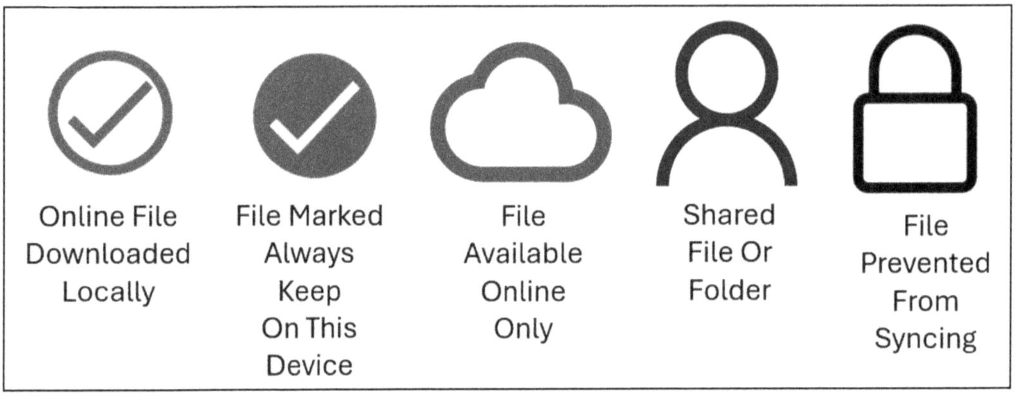

Figure 4.9

Now if you were to create a new file or folder in the OneDrive folder on your computer or edit a file within this folder, it would be synchronized to your online storage.

OneDrive App Settings

Once the OneDrive desktop app is running, you should see it in your Windows system tray on the right side of the taskbar. You can then click on it to see the status of any file synchronizations. At the top of the app, you will see an icon that you can click on the go to the OneDrive settings. You will also have icons at the bottom that you can click on to open your local OneDrive folder, go to the OneDrive website or view any deleted files in the OneDrive Recycle bin.

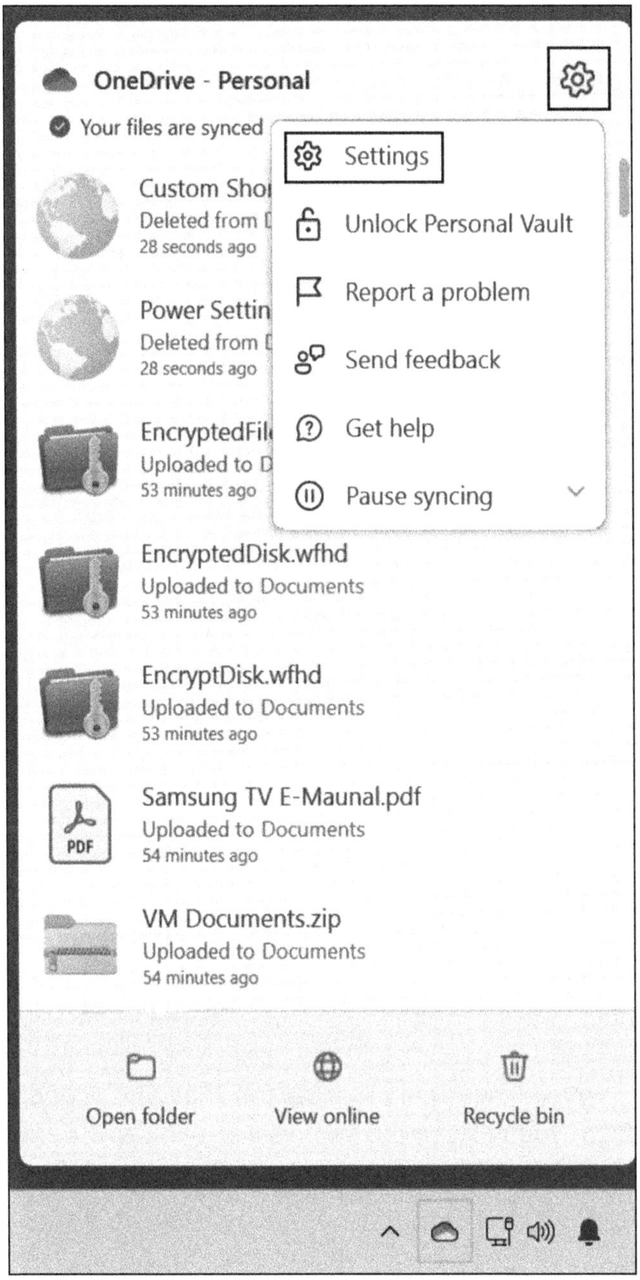

Figure 4.10

Once you are in the OneDrive settings, you can then do things such as change your sync and backup settings, view your account information, and change what notifications are shown from the OneDrive app.

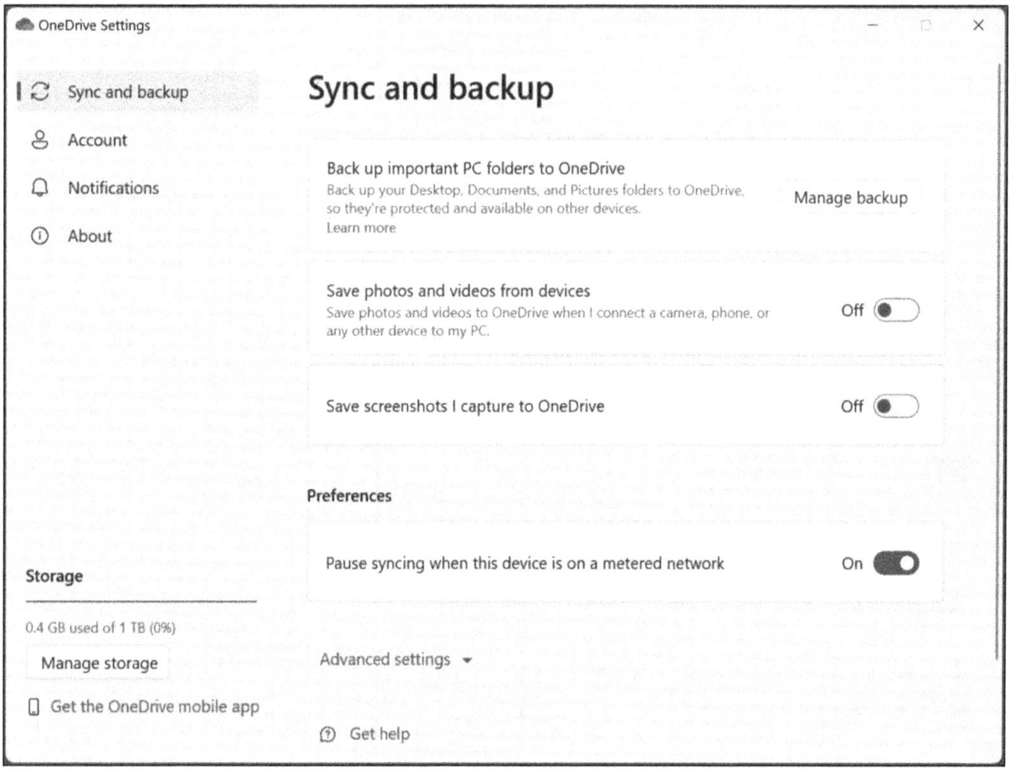

Figure 4.11

Adding or Removing Folders to Be Synchronized

When it comes to changing what folders are synchronized between the OneDrive client and the OneDrive website, you are a bit limited, but you still have several options that might fit your needs.

If you look back at figure 4.11, you will see there is a button that says *Manage backup*. If you click on this button, you will see the same screen you saw during the initial OneDrive client setup (Figure 4.12).

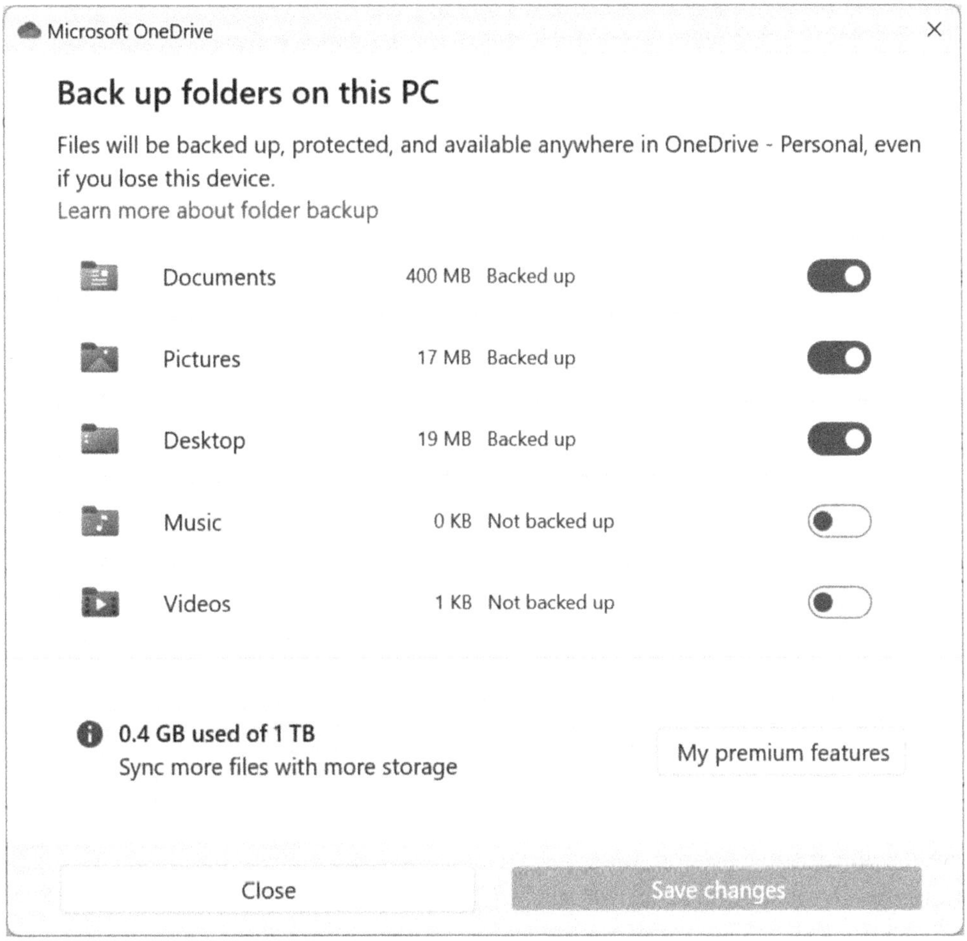

Figure 4.12

From here, you can select additional folders to be backed up or deselect folders you no longer want to be backed up.

Another option is to go to the *Account* section in the OneDrive settings and click the *Choose folders* button.

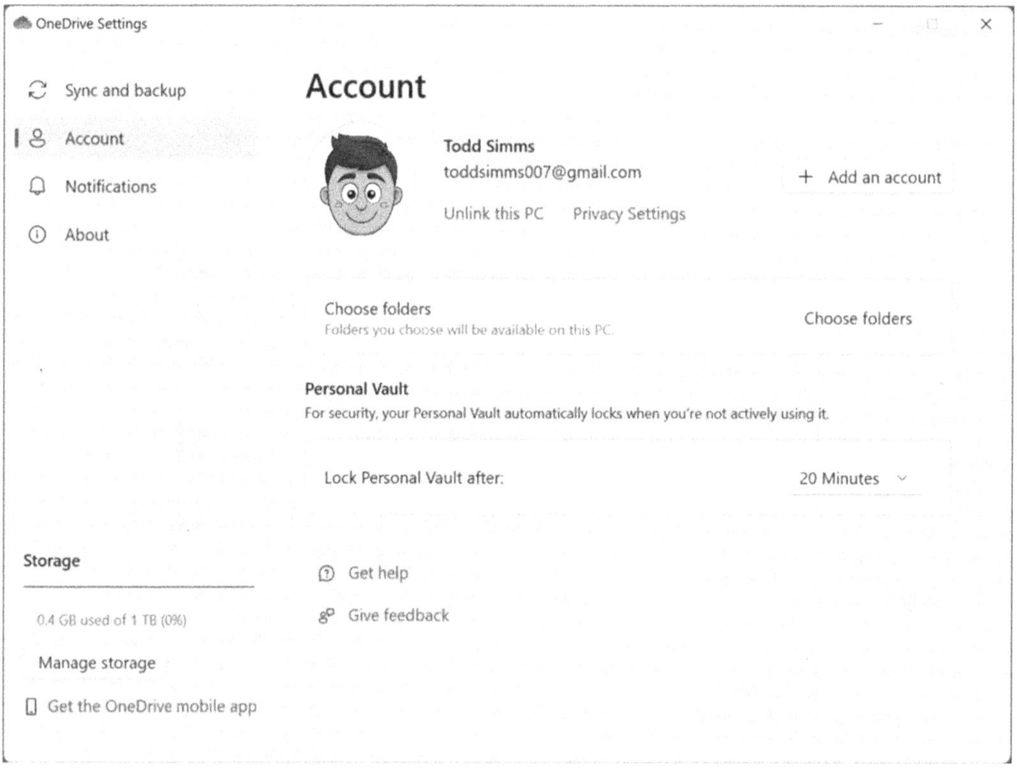

Figure 4.13

Here you will be able to fine tune which of your online files and folders will be available locally on your computer within your OneDrive folder. When you have files and folders set to be locally available, this means you will still be able to access them even if you do not have an internet connection or access to your OneDrive account online.

As you can see in Figure 4.14, there are some folders that you cannot disable indicated by the greyed out checkbox. This is because these folders were selected during the backup configuration. If you were to disable the backup of these folders, then you would be able to check or uncheck the box next to those folders.

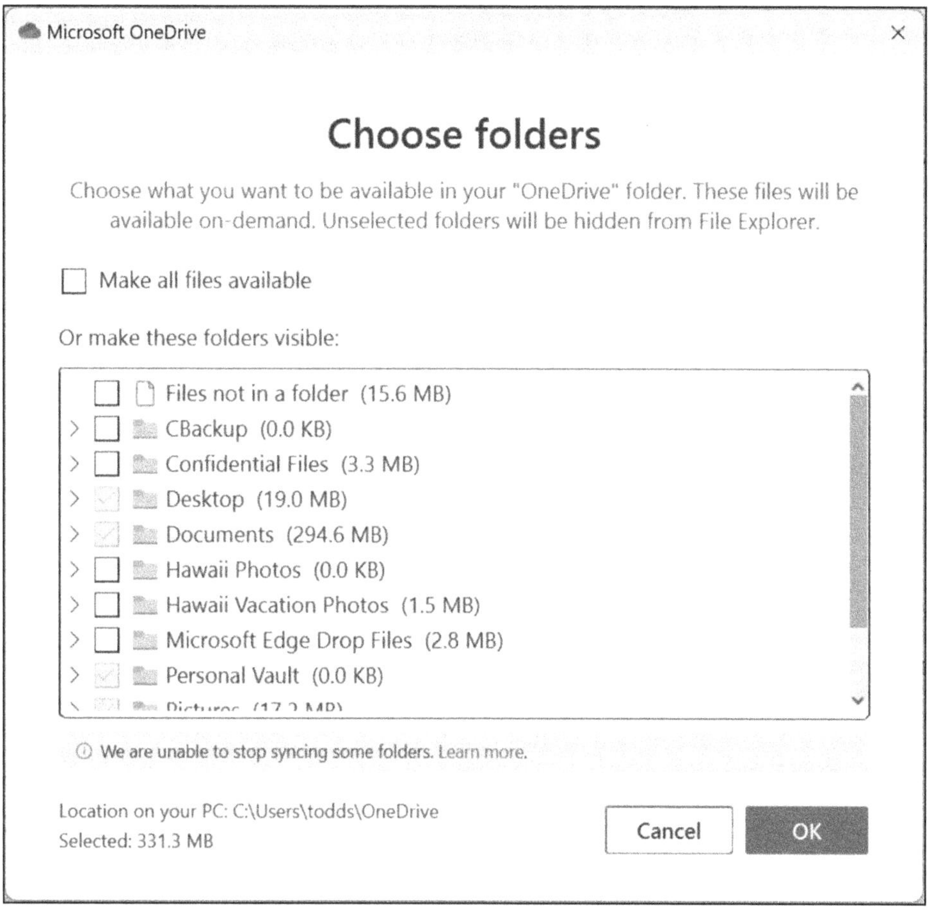

Figure 4.14

Checking Your Available Storage Space

Your OneDrive account has a limit as to how much data you can store within it. This is similar to the hard drive in your computer which can only hold so many files and folders before it gets full.

How much space you have for storing files and folders online will be determined by what type of OneDrive account you have. I discussed the various OneDrive plans back in Chapter 1, but you can also view your total space allocation by looking at the lower left corner of the OneDrive web interface (Figure 4.15) or by going to the settings from the OneDrive app (Figure 4.16).

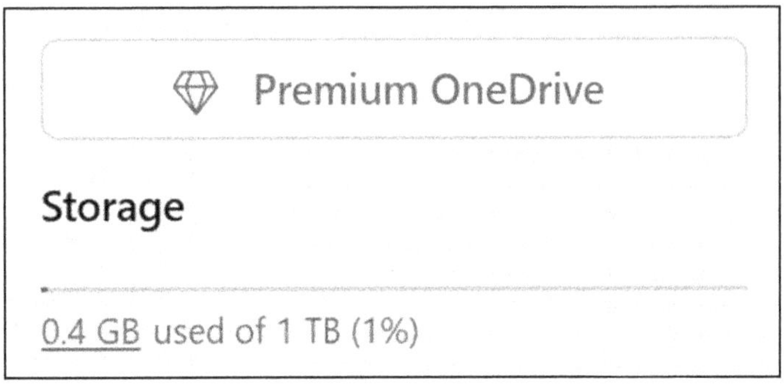

Figure 4.15

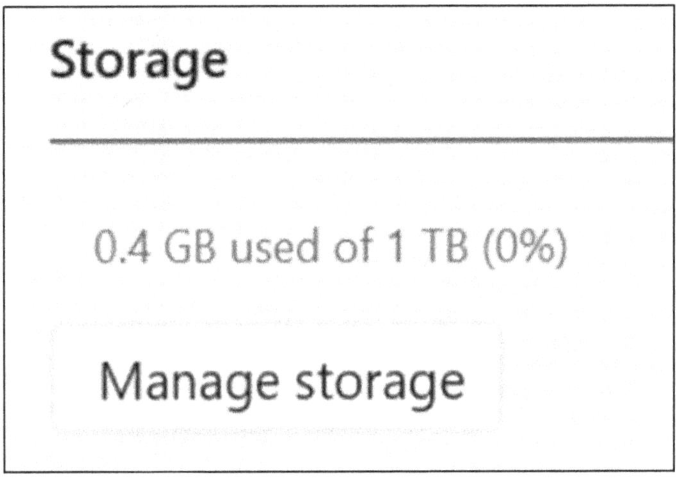

Figure 4.16

Once you are in your storage settings, you will see how much space you have used with your OneDrive files as well as your Microsoft Outlook account, assuming you use one.

As you can see in Figure 4.17, there is a section labeled *Free up space* that gives you some areas where you can do some cleanup in case you are running out of room. It will also show you which subscription plan you are using, if any. You can also view details about your Microsoft account from here by clicking on the *View* link.

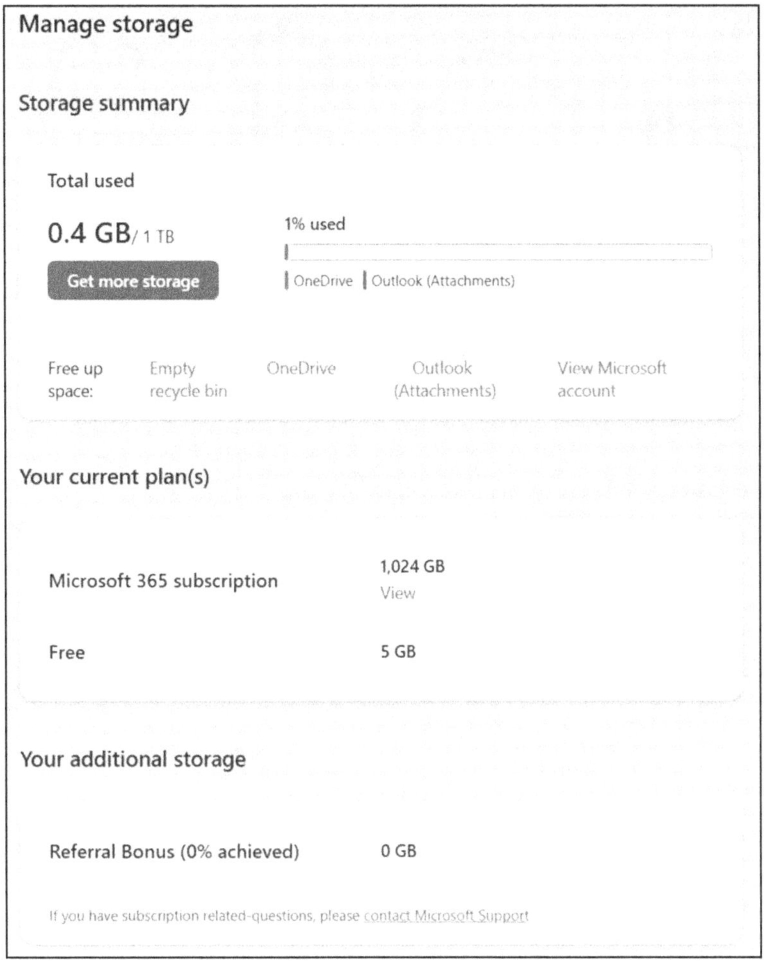

Figure 4.17

Offline vs Online Files (Files on Demand)

If you are using the OneDrive client, then you will have the option to decide if you want to keep your file stored locally or only in the cloud. The advantage to storing them locally is that if you lose your internet connection or the OneDrive site is down, you will still have access to your files.

If you use the online only option, then that saves you disk space by storing your files only on the OneDrive website. Then the files are downloaded to your computer as you need them (on demand).

These options can be assigned to all your files or just the ones that you choose. If you remember the graphic from the beginning of this chapter, you can see what icon is associated with what file status.

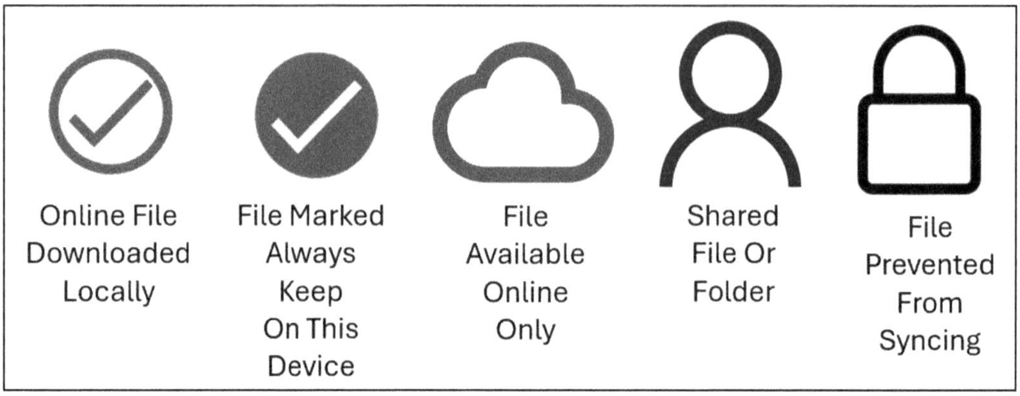

Figure 4.18

Within the OneDrive settings under *Sync and backup*, there is a section labeled *Files On-Demand*. If you want to configure all your files so they are kept online OR on your PC, you can do so from here.

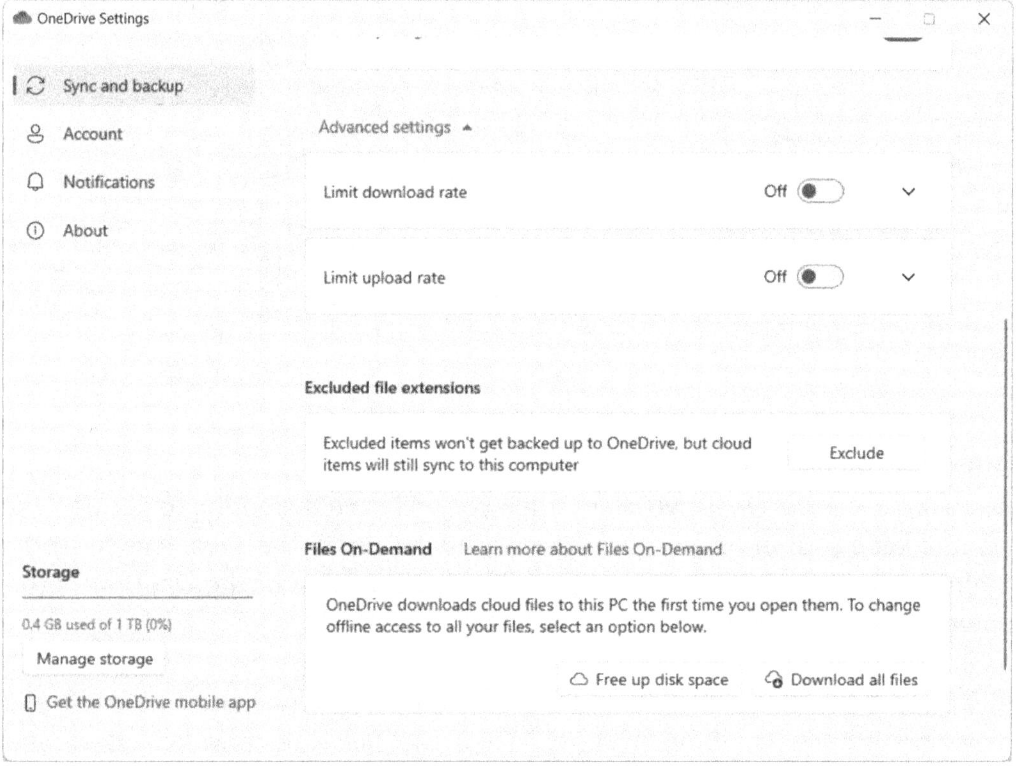

Figure 4.19

Another option is to open the OneDrive folder on your computer and there you can see the status of your files. Figure 4.20 shows a Brochure file as being an online file that was downloaded locally.

Figure 4.20

If I were to right click on the file, I have the option to always keep it on this device (local) or always keep it online (Free up space).

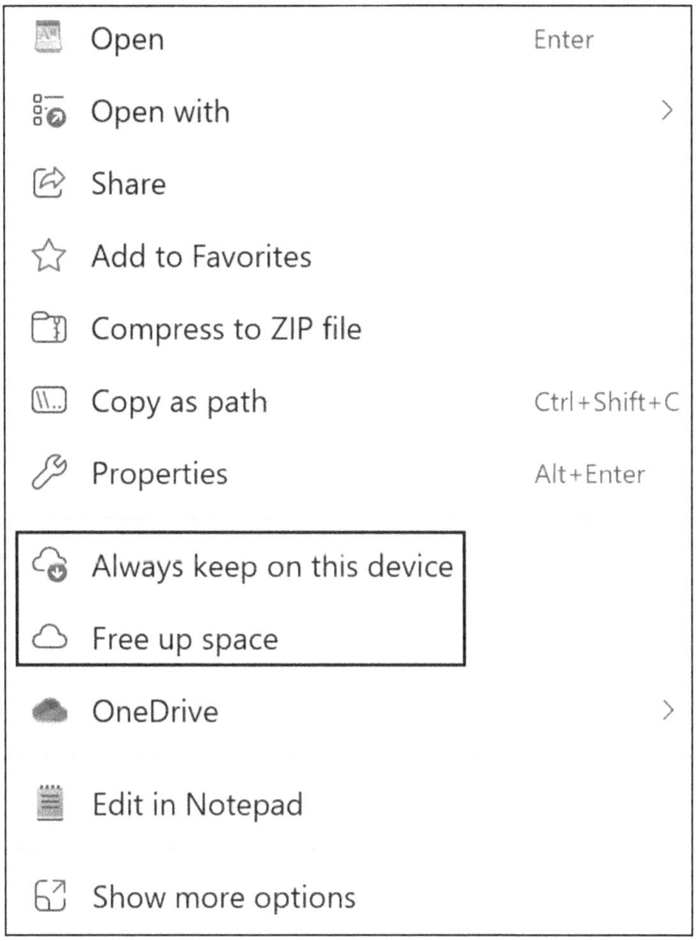

Figure 4.21

If I choose the Always keep on this device option, you can see the icon next to the file name changes accordingly.

Figure 4.22

Now when I change it to use the Free up space option, the icon changes once again to match its new status.

Figure 4.23

Chapter 5 – Sharing Files and Folders

One of the more common uses for cloud storage services such as OneDrive, Dropbox and Google Drive is to share files and folders with other people so they can do things such as view your photos or collaborate with you on documents or other types of files. You do not need to take advantage of this sharing feature to use OneDrive, but it can come in very handy when you want to send someone a file or allow someone to work on a document without having to email it to them.

Sharing Files and Folders

The process for sharing files is almost identical to that of sharing folders except when you share a folder, the people you share it with have access to the files within that folder. So, if you do not want other users to see all the files in a folder, you should either move the other files to a different folder or create a new shared folder and move or copy the files you want them to see into it.

To share a file or folder, you can either right click on it or click on the ellipsis next to its name and choose the *Share* option. The *Manage access* option can be used to adjust permissions on shared files and folders after you have already shared them. You can select more than one file or folder at a time to share.

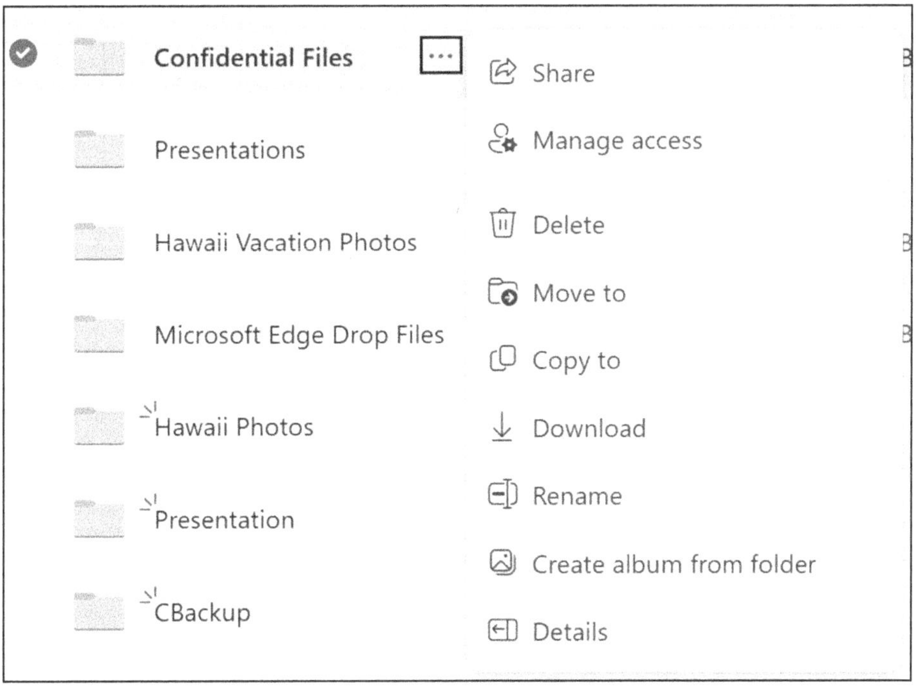

Figure 5.1

Once you click on Share, you will be able to type in the email address or addresses of those who you want to share the file or folder with. You can then type in a message that will be sent with the invitation to the shared file or folder.

The *Copy link* option at the bottom can be used to create a link to the shared file or folder that can be emailed to people or shared in other apps such as instant messaging programs.

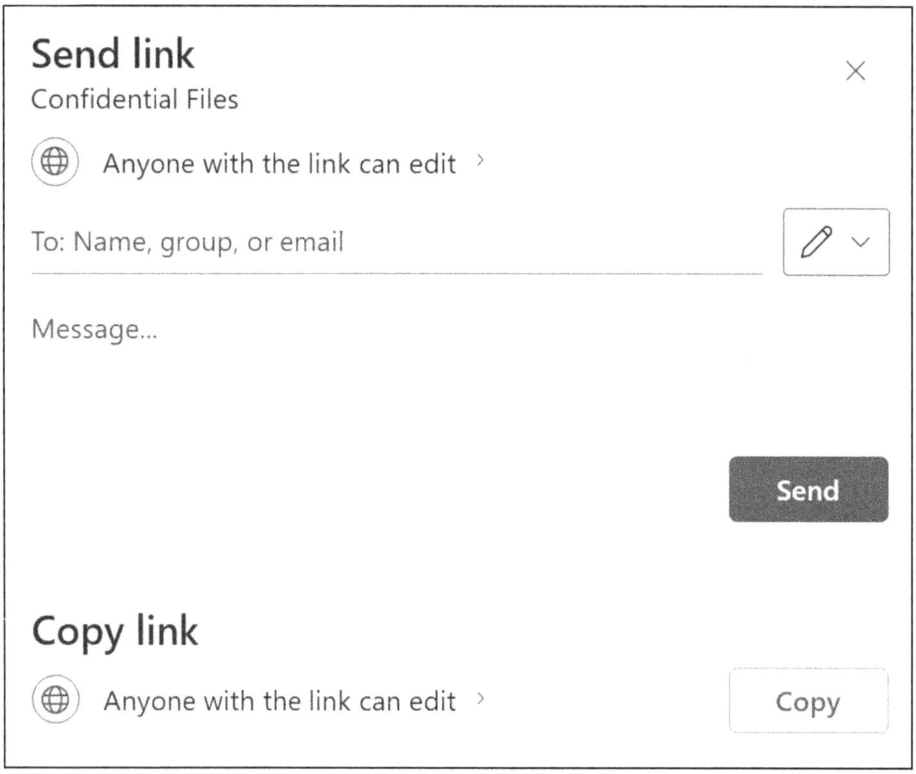

Figure 5.2

If you click on the edit pencil icon, you can change the permission level from editor to viewer in case you do not want anyone to be able to make changes to your files.

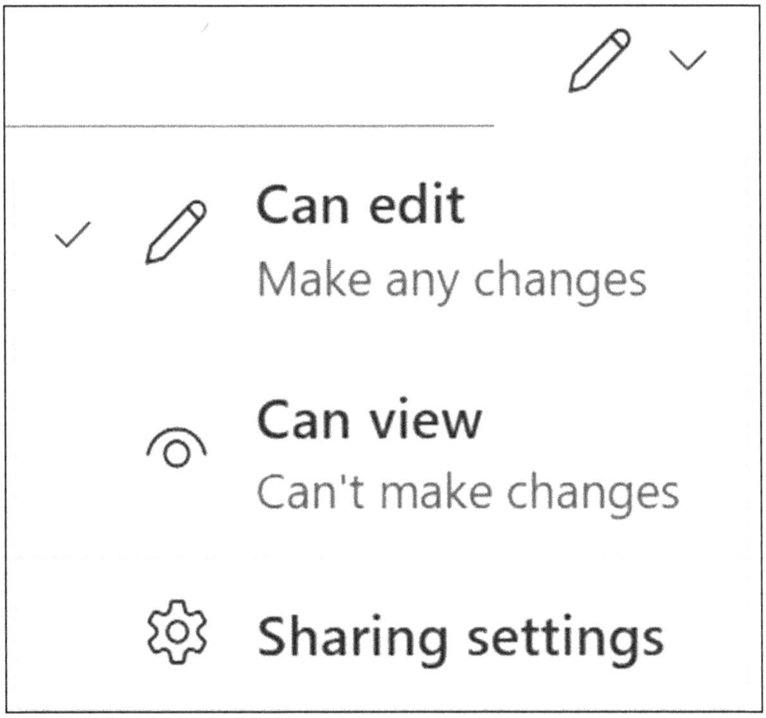

Figure 5.3

If you click on the arrow to the right of *Anyone with the link can edit* or the *Sharing settings* option from Figure 5.3, you will then be able to configure additional settings such as setting an expiration date or password on the shared file or folder.

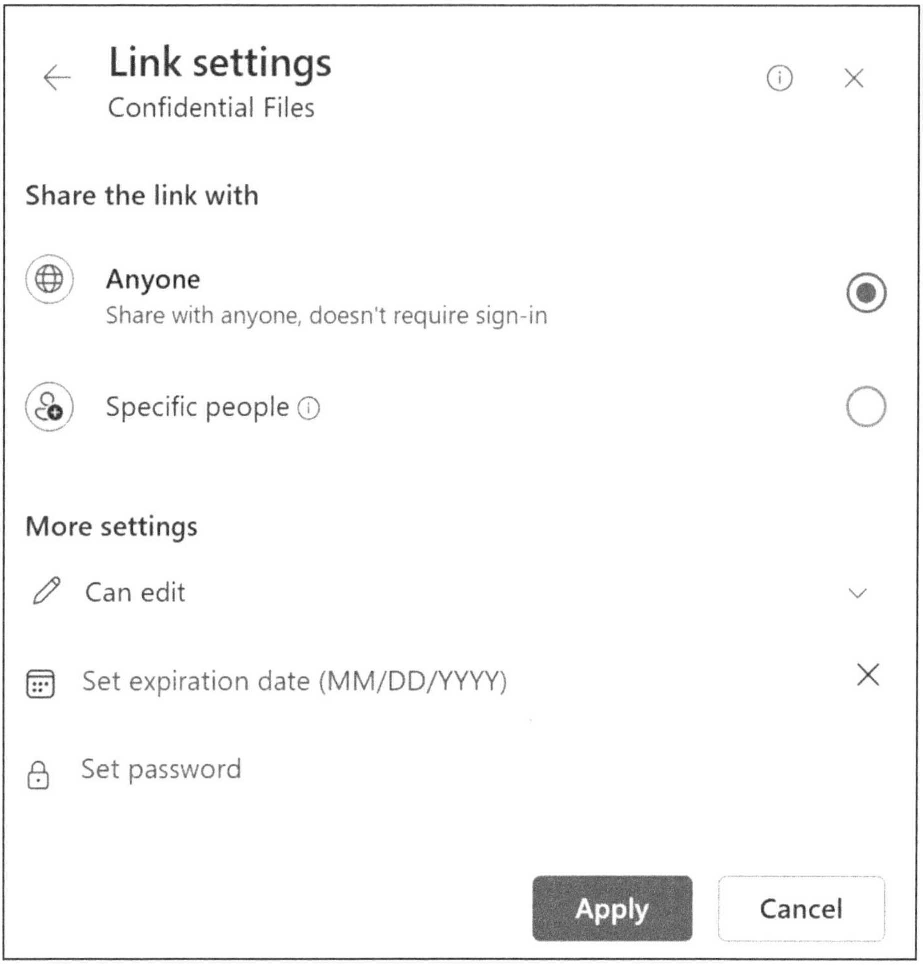

Figure 5.4

I will now put in Cindy's email address and add a message to be sent with the invitation. I will also add a password to the shared folder to keep it more secure in case someone gets a hold of Cindy's email with the shared folder invitation.

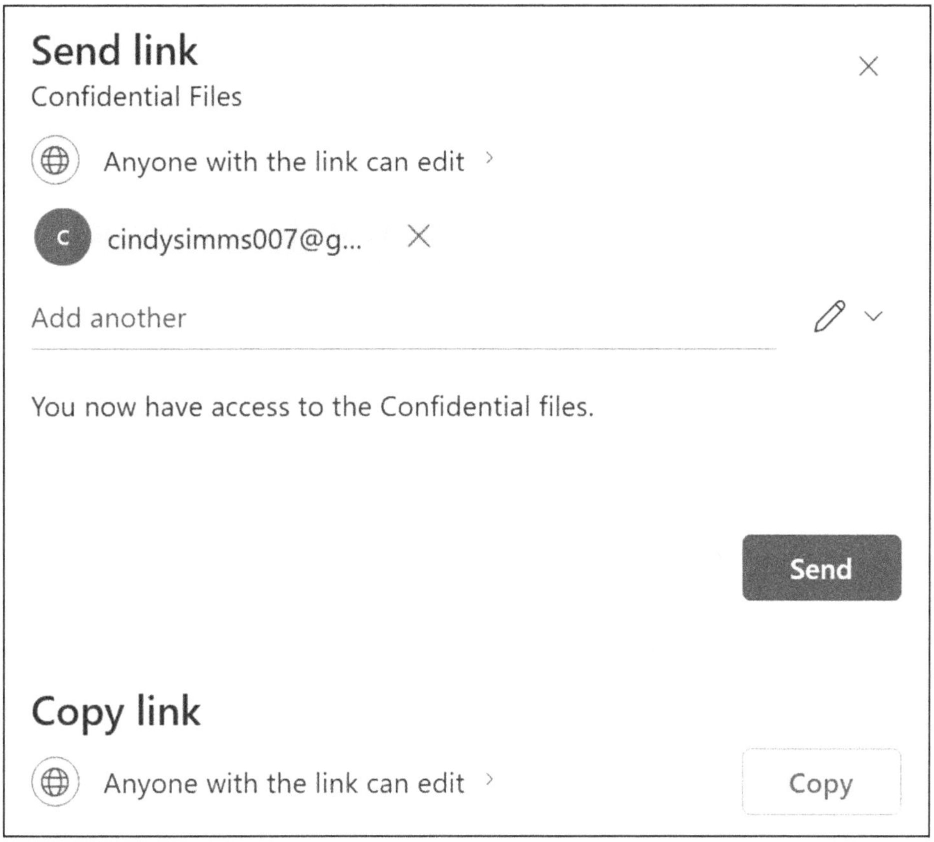

Figure 5.5

Now that I have added a password to the share, I now have a lock icon on the main share screen and if I hover my mouse over it, I will be informed that I need to share the password with the person I am sharing the folder with.

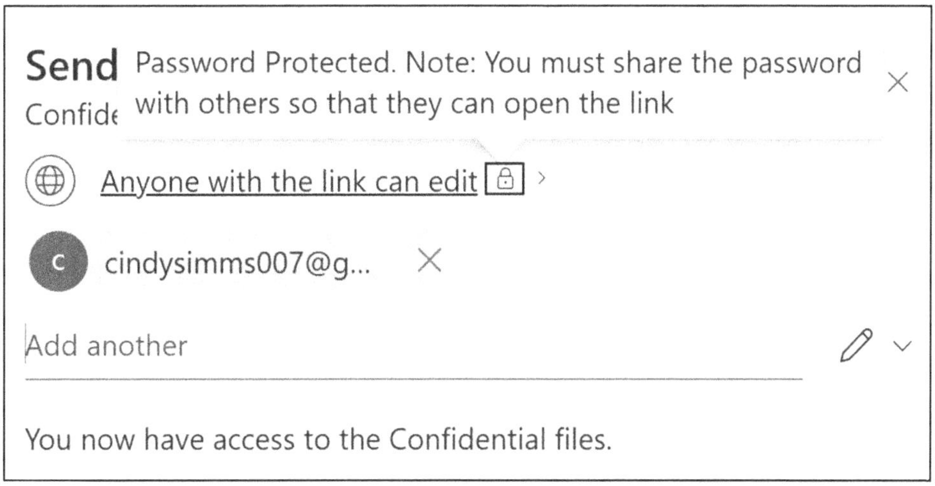

Figure 5.6

Figure 5.7 shows how the email about the shared file invitation will look when received by Cindy.

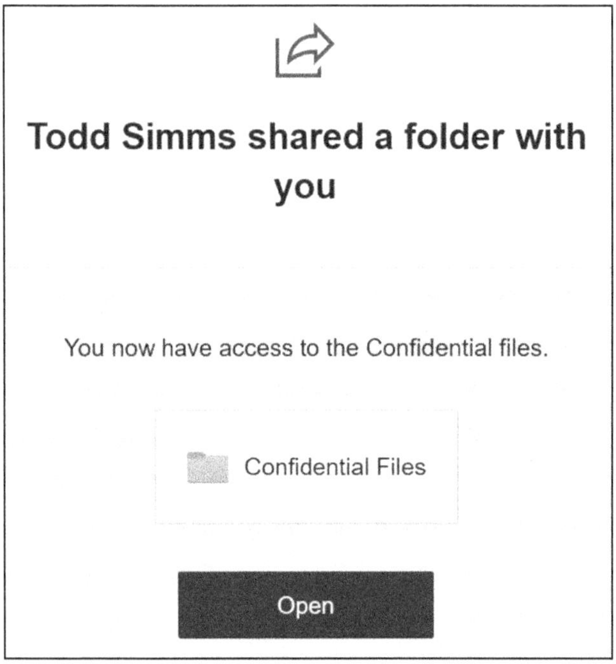

Figure 5.7

When she clicks on the *Open* button, she will need to type in the password assigned to the shared folder.

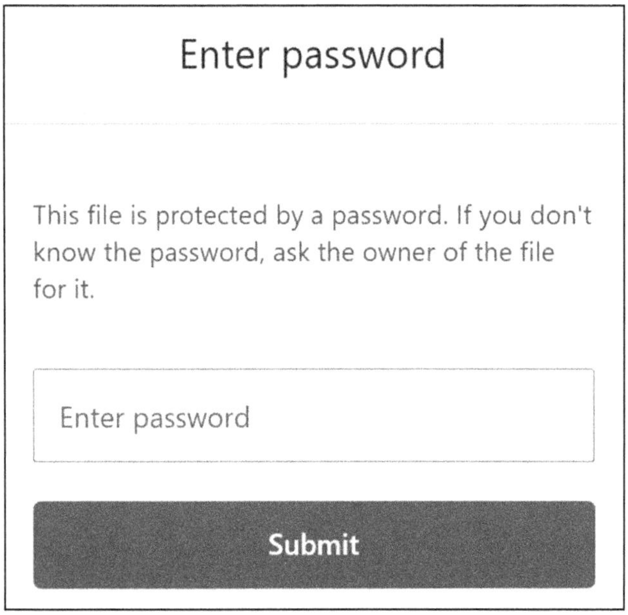

Figure 5.8

Once Cindy enters the password, she will then be able to see the shared folder and its contents without needing to log into her own OneDrive account. If you look at the folders, you will see that there is a sharing icon on each folder.

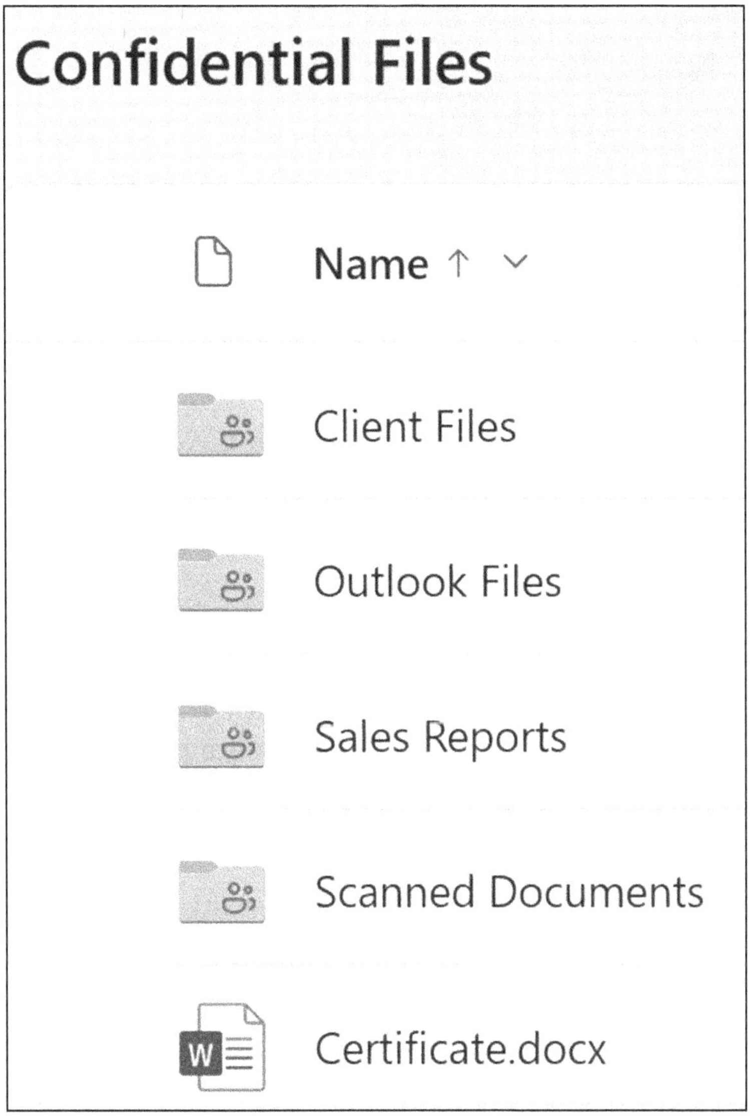

Figure 5.9

Now that the folder has been shared, Todd will see a shared folder icon on the Confidential Files folder on his computer.

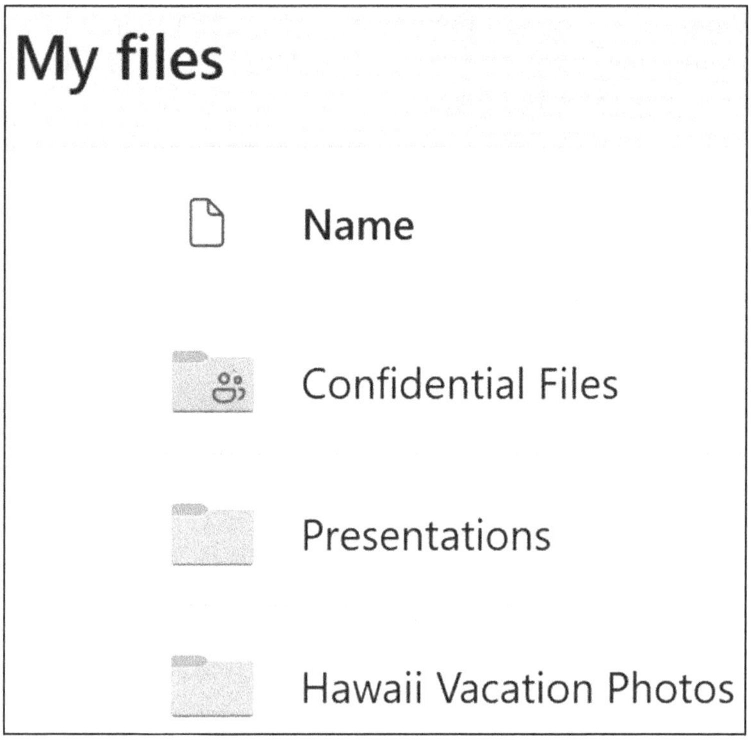

Figure 5.10

Now Cindy can view and open any file or folder within the shared Confidential Files folder since she has edit permission. She can even add her own files or subfolders if needed. But in order to add new files or folders, she will need to sign into her own OneDrive account so that she can be associated with any new items she adds to this shared folder.

Checking Share Activity

To view any files and folders that you have shared or that others have shared with you, simply go to the *Shared* section and then select either *With you* or *By you* at the top.

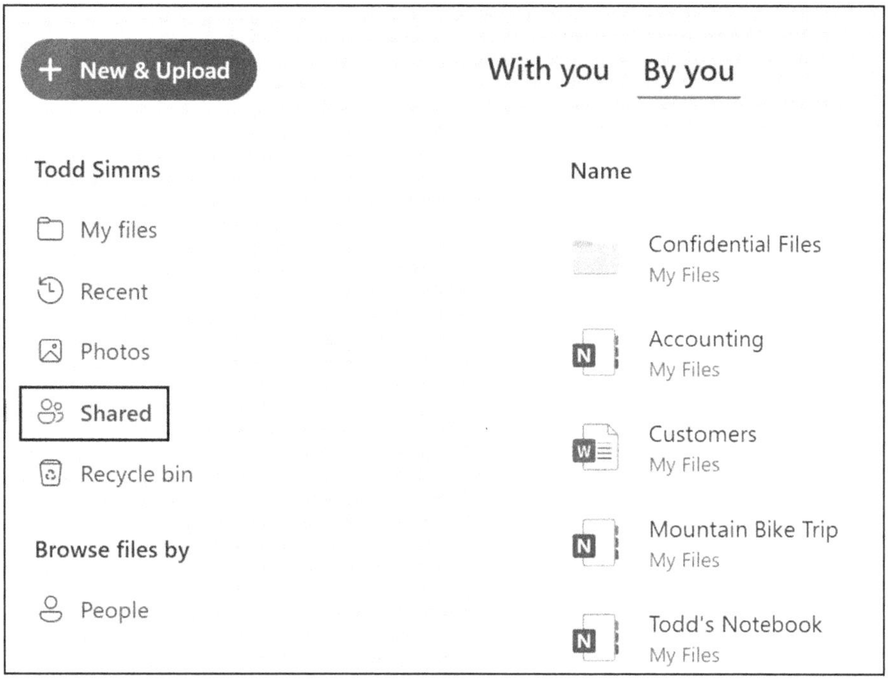

Figure 5.11

To view details about a shared file or folder, you can click on the ellipsis next to its name and choose the *Manage access* option. You will then be able to view and edit the permissions for your shared files and folders as well as any shared links you have made for them.

Figure 5.12

To check the status of a shared file or folder, you can open the Details pane and see when a file was modified. Figure 5.13 shows that a Word document was created by Todd on June 28th and then edited by both Todd and Cindy today.

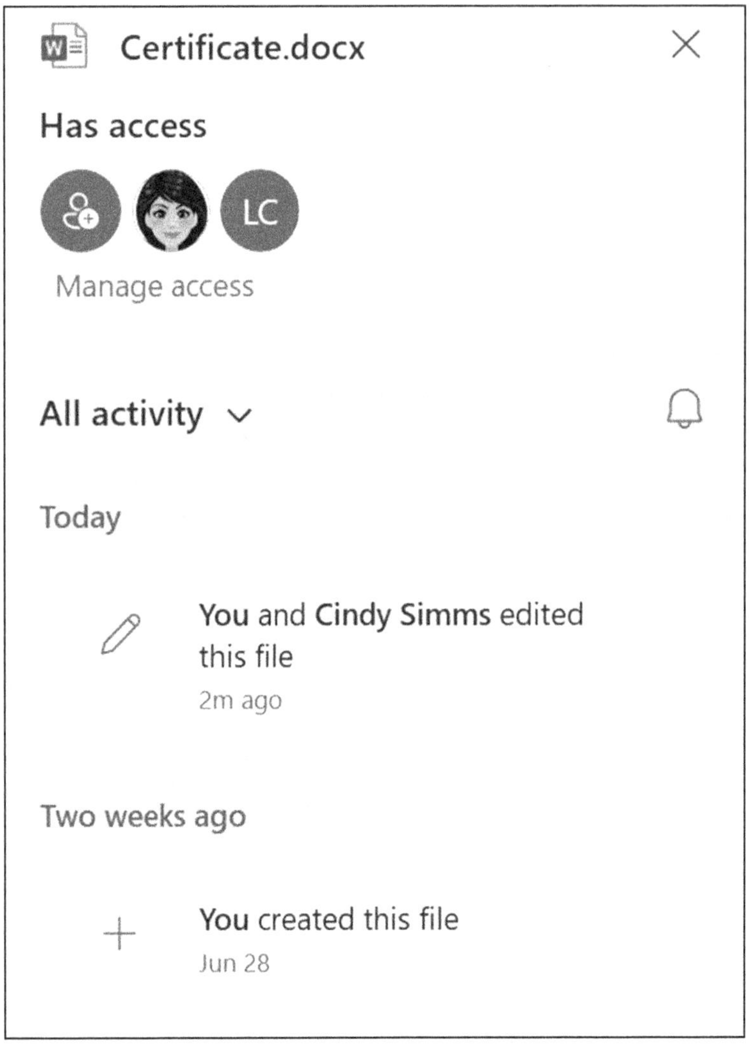

Figure 5.13

Figure 5.14 shows that a file was created by Cindy within a folder that was shared with her by Todd.

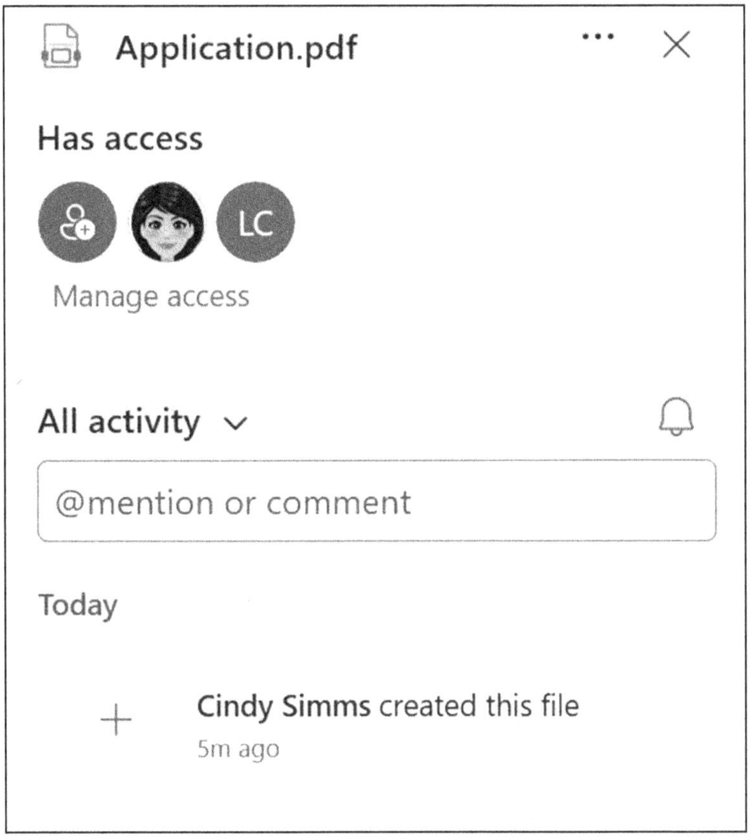

Figure 5.14

As you can see, you do not get much in the way of specific details when it comes to your shared files and folders, but I suppose it is better than nothing!

Viewing Files and Folders Shared with You

Another place to see what files are shared with you is to go to the *People* section. This area will show the names of those who are sharing the files as well as what files and folders they are sharing.

Figure 5.15

If you have multiple people sharing with you, then you can click on their name to only see files and folders shared by that person.

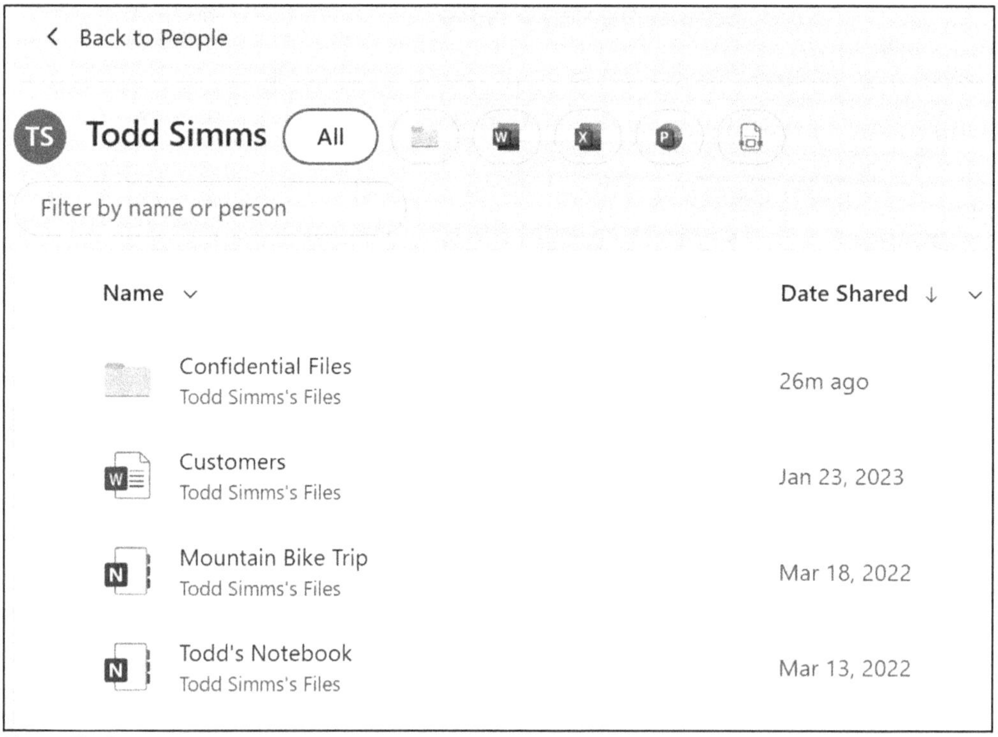

Figure 5.16

While viewing these shared files and folders, you can click on the ellipsis next to one to see some actions that you can take on this shared item. Figure 5.17 shows the options when viewing a shared folder.

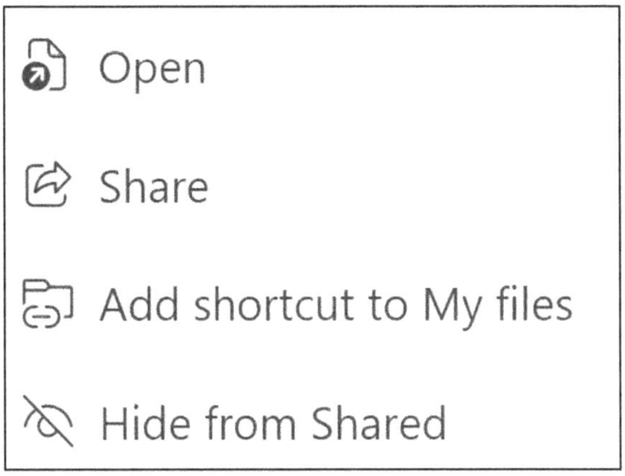

Figure 5.17

Figure 5.18 shows the options for a shared Word document.

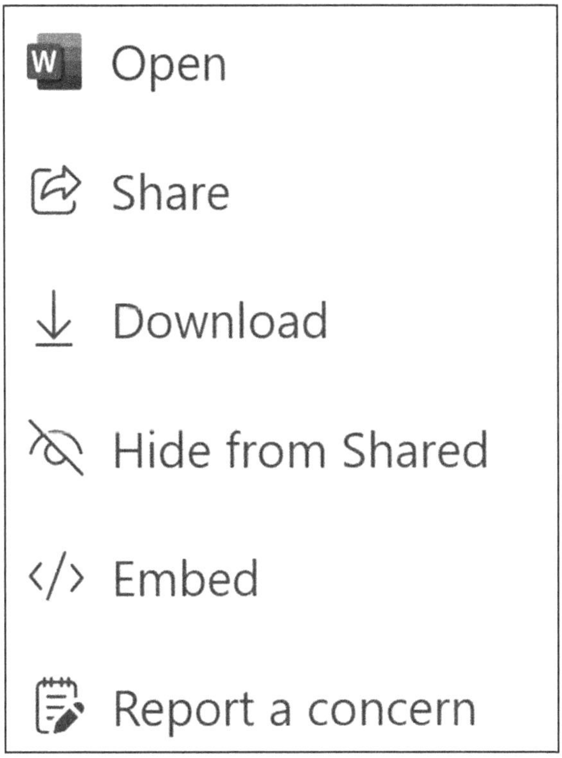

Figure 5.18

Changing Permissions and Stopping Sharing

If you need to make any changes to the sharing permission on your files and folders or even remove access altogether, you can easily do so by going back to the Share or Manage access settings for that item.

You can then click on the pencil edit icon next to the user you want to change or remove to view their access level.

Figure 5.19

You don't have too many options when it comes to sharing with OneDrive so you can either change their access to view or edit or click on the *Remove direct access* option to un-share the file or folder with them.

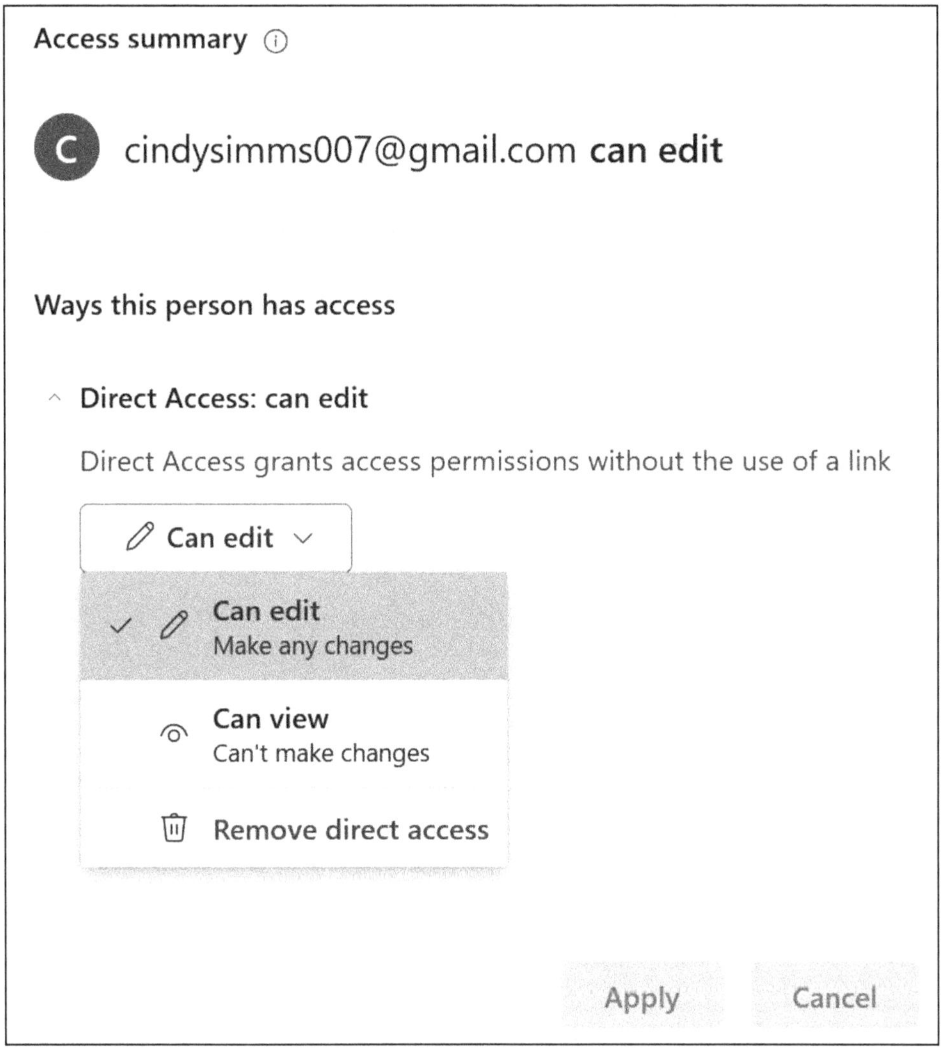

Figure 5.20

If you change or remove access to a folder, it will affect all the files and subfolders within that shared folder.

Chapter 6 – OneDrive Settings & Preferences

The OneDrive website has a variety of settings that you can use to configure how OneDrive works for you. It is broken down into several categories and in this chapter, I will be discussing many of these options as well as how you can do things such as configure your Microsoft Profile as well as get additional help if needed.

OneDrive Website Options

The OneDrive website has a variety of settings that you can configure to customize your cloud storage experience. To get to these settings, simply click on the gear icon at the upper right corner of the page and then choose *Options*.

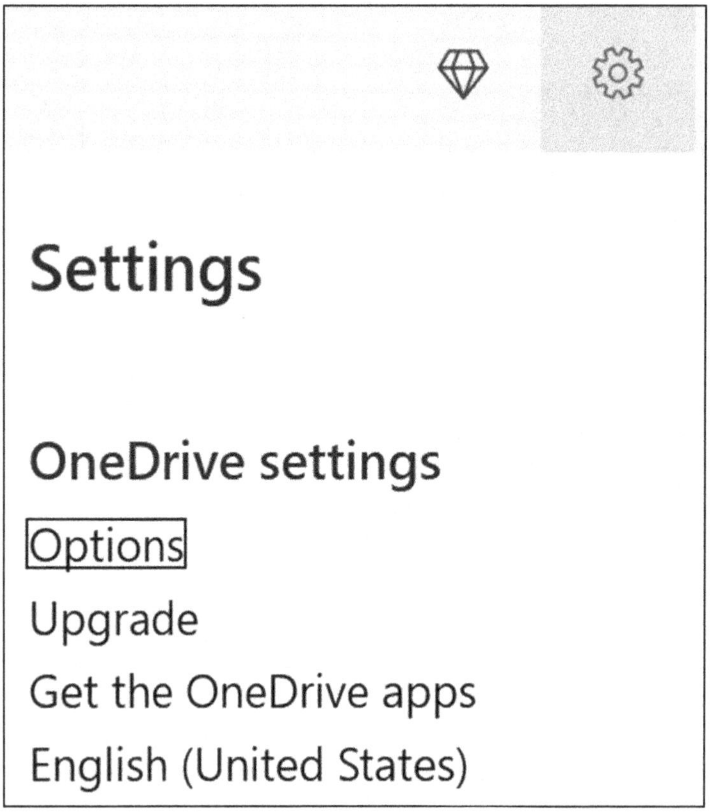

Figure 6.1

You will then see what available options you can configure. Some of these settings have already been discussed but I will now go over some of the other options that I feel are important to know about.

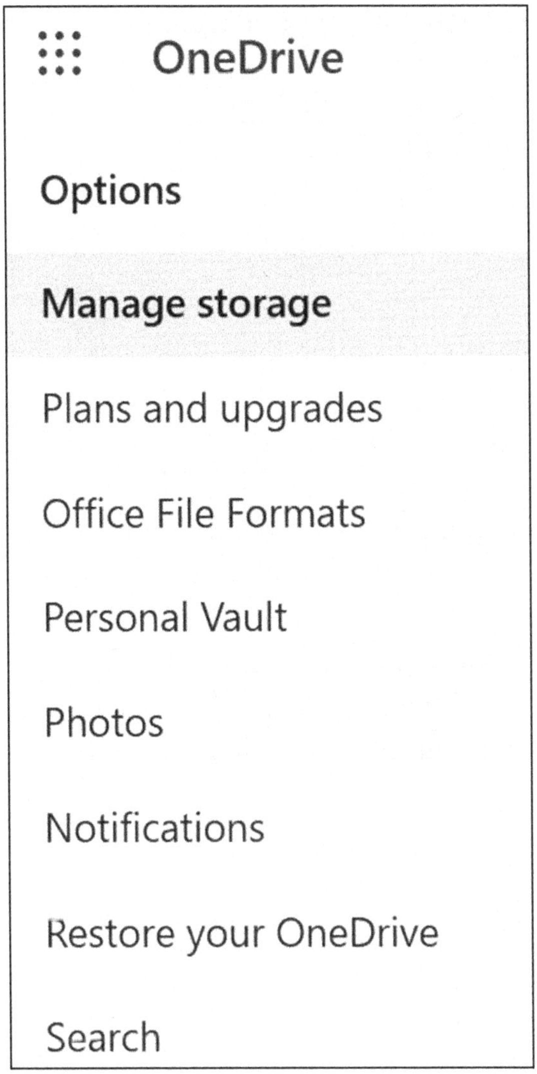

Figure 6.2

Manage Storage
This section will show you the storage you have available with your OneDrive and Outlook email account. I went over this information in Chapter 4.

Plans and Upgrades
If you would like to upgrade your account to get additional storage or access to the Microsoft 365 apps such as Word and Excel, you can do so from here.

Office File Formats
By default, OneDrive will use the Microsoft Office Open XML format for documents that you create within your OneDrive account. This is because

OneDrive is owned by Microsoft and therefore, they are going to use their own format for new documents by default.

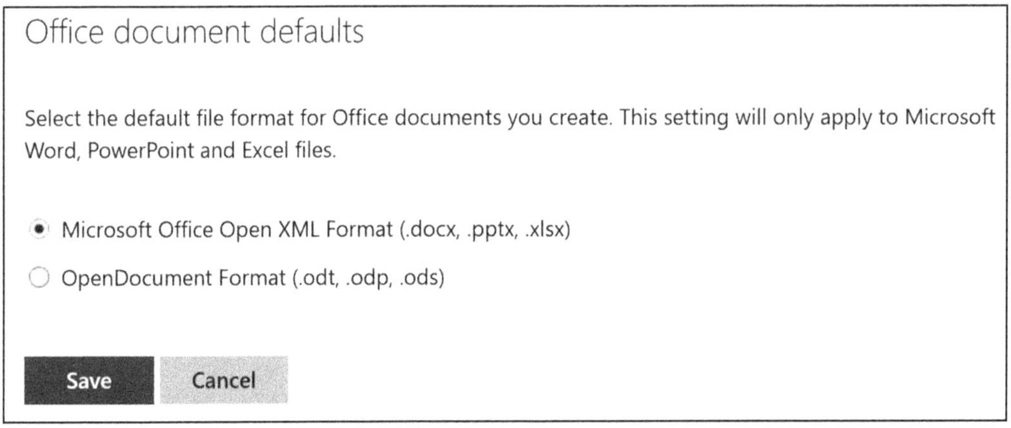

Figure 6.3

Personal Vault

As you saw in Chapter 4, you need to verify your identity before you can open your Personal Vault and view your secure files and folders. If you need to change the authentication method used for accessing your Personal Vault or change your password, you can do so from here.

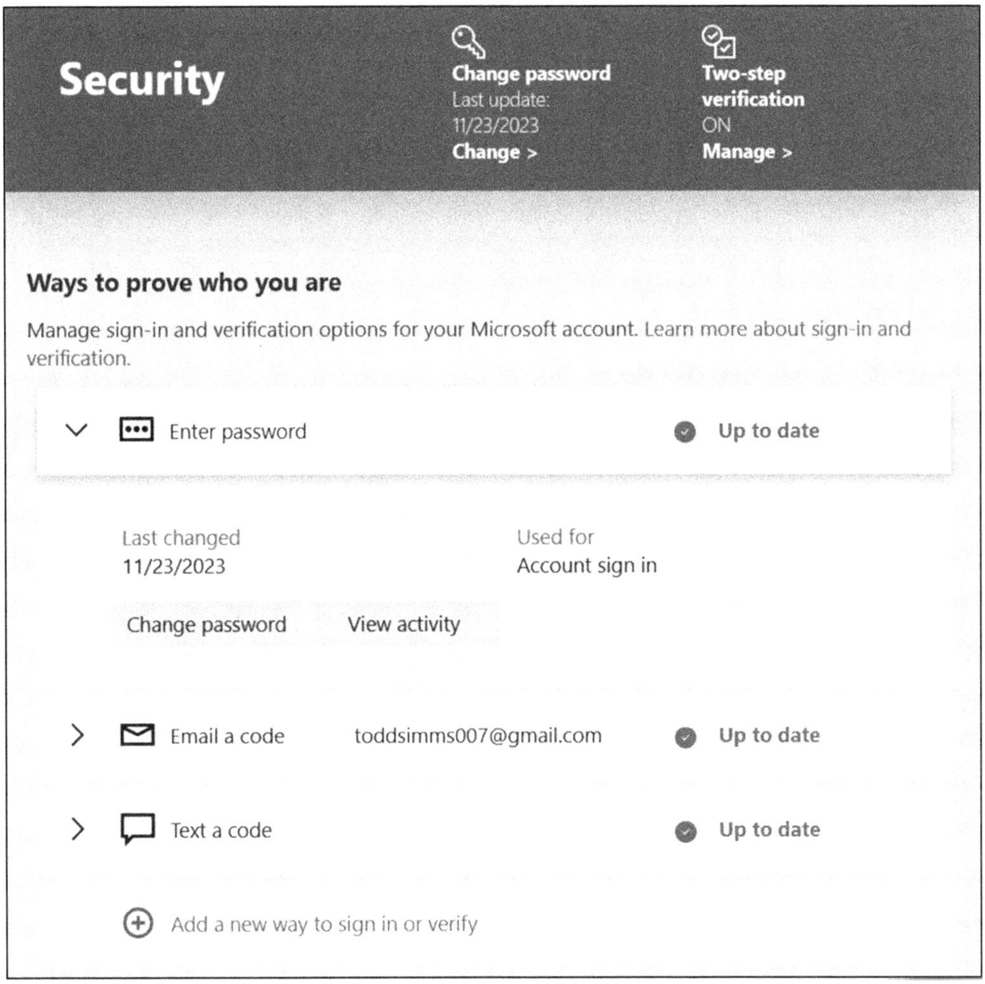

Figure 6.4

Photos

Since OneDrive has a Photos section, they will try and tag your photos by default so when you go to the Explore section for example, it will show your photos in categories based on how they were tagged. You may find that your photos are not being tagged accurately so you can come here and disable the tagging feature if desired.

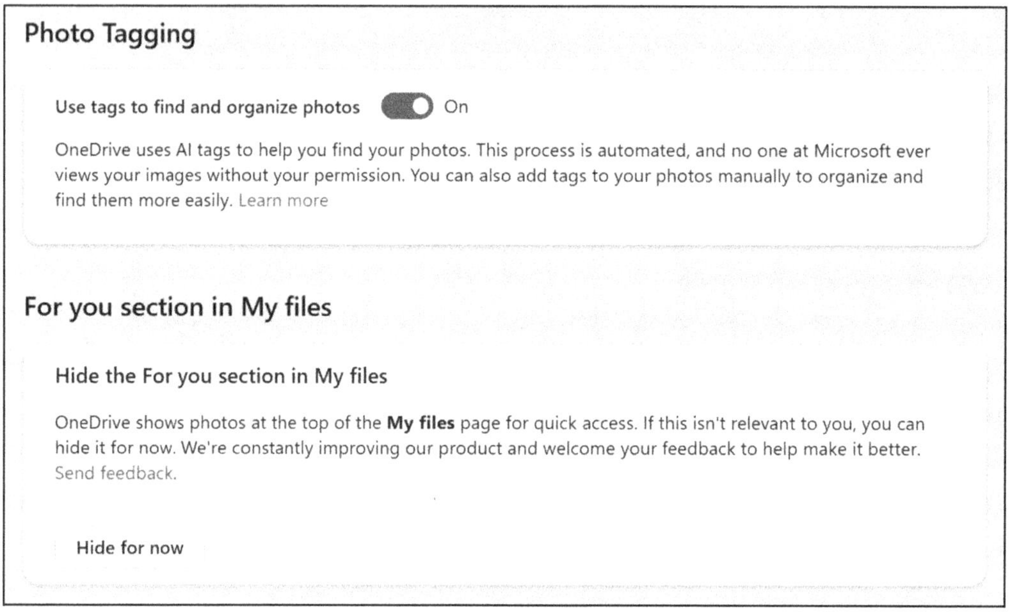

Figure 6.5

Notifications

If you find that you are getting too many emails from Microsoft about your OneDrive account, you can come here to disable some or all these email notifications.

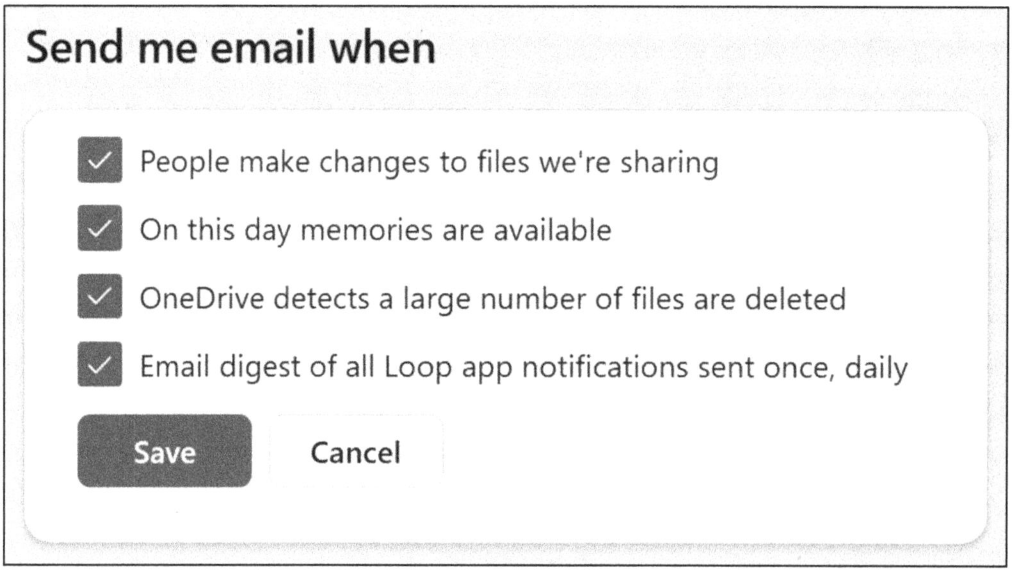

Figure 6.6

Restore your OneDrive

The Restore your OneDrive setting is a feature that allows you to recover your entire OneDrive account to a previous state. This can be particularly useful in cases of accidental deletion, file corruption, ransomware attacks, or other data loss scenarios.

To use this option, you will need to verify your identity just like you do when accessing the Personal Vault.

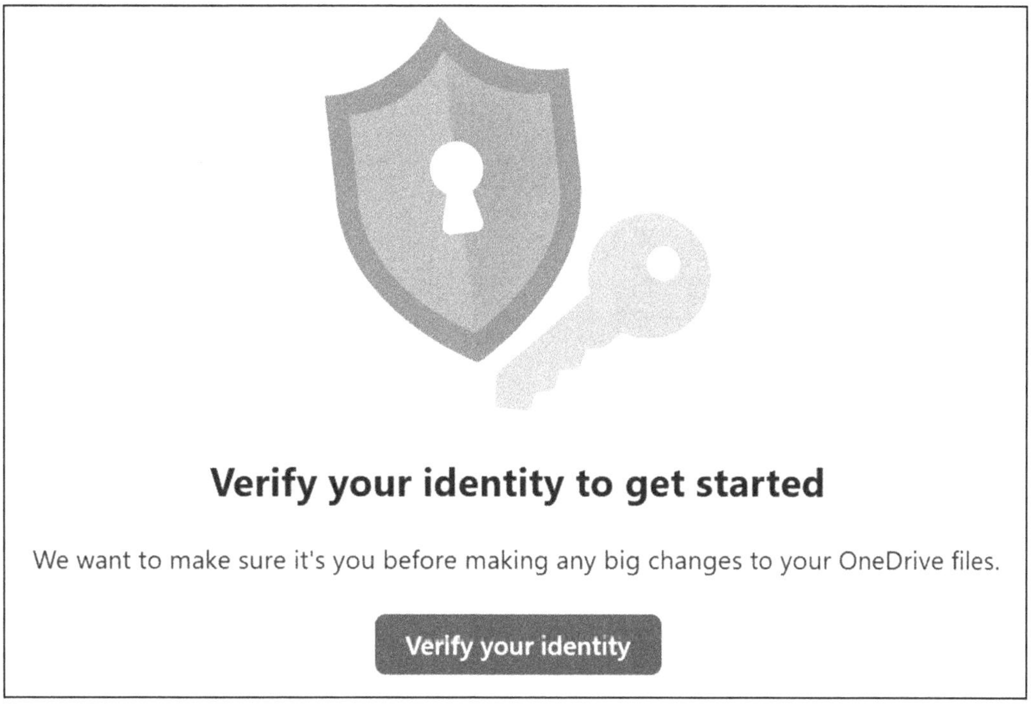

Figure 6.7

Then you will be able to choose a recovery period. Your options will be yesterday, one week, three weeks, or a custom date. Then you can choose which actions you want to undo from the list below. Be careful using this feature because if you don't do it correctly, you risk losing your files for good. Plus you need to keep in mind that your files will be reverted back to the date you choose so anything done after that will be lost.

Figure 6.8

Search

There is not much you can do here when it comes to search settings except enable the search history or clear the search history if you have already been using it.

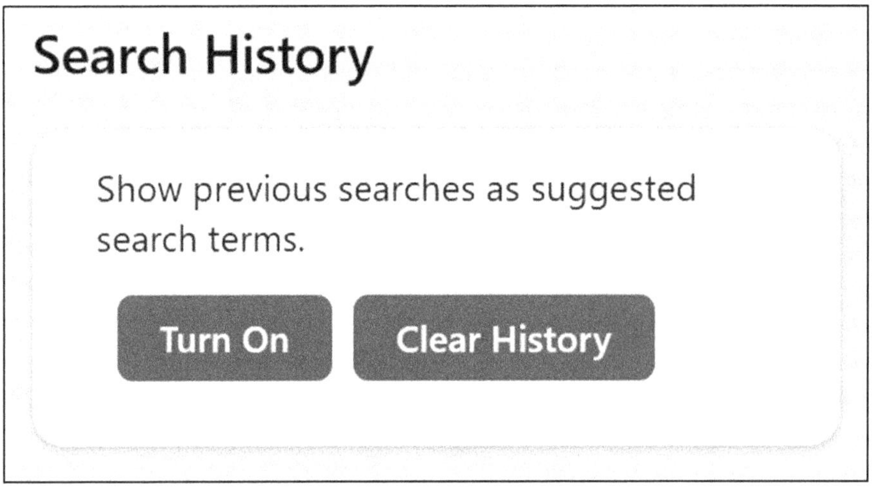

Figure 6.9

Microsoft Account & Profile

I wanted to briefly go over some of the things you will find when you view your Microsoft account or profile since you may need to go there at some point to view information about your account or make changes.

If you click on your profile picture (or letter if you don't have one), you can choose *My Microsoft Account* or *My profile* from the links that appear to view these options. Whichever one you choose, you can get to the other settings from the same page.

Figure 6.10

The *Your info* screen shows you details about your account such as your birthdate, email address, and phone number. If you want to add a profile picture to your account, you can do so from here and it will show up when you share files and folders with other people.

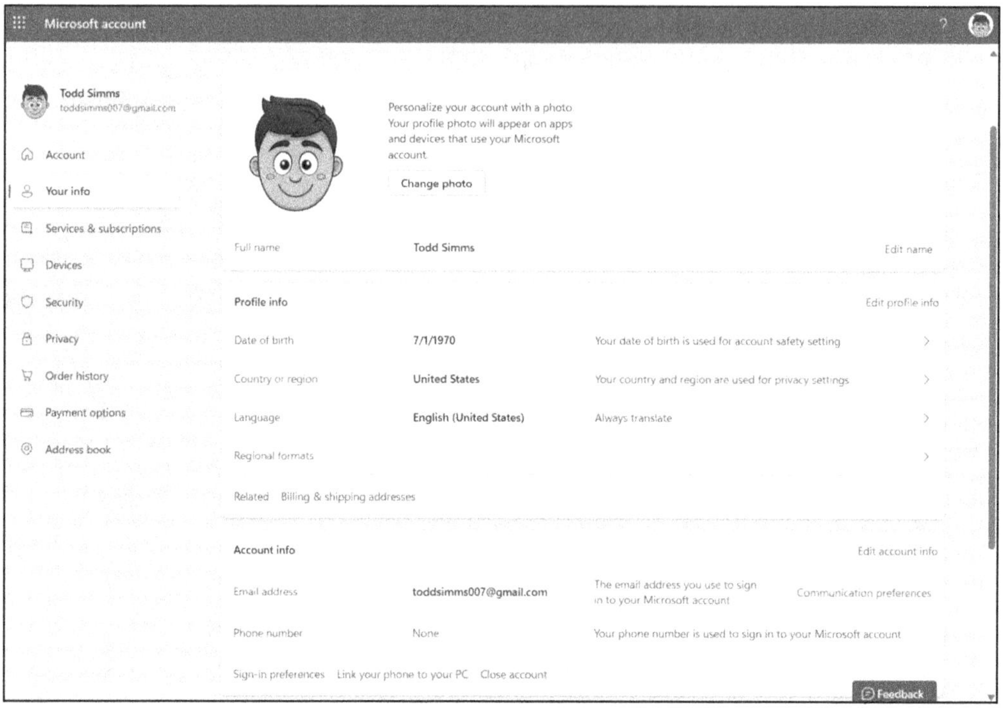

Figure 6.11

The *Services & subscriptions* section will show you details about your account for things such as Microsoft 365 and allow you to install the desktop apps if you have the right subscription type. You can also view details about your subscriptions in the *Order history* section.

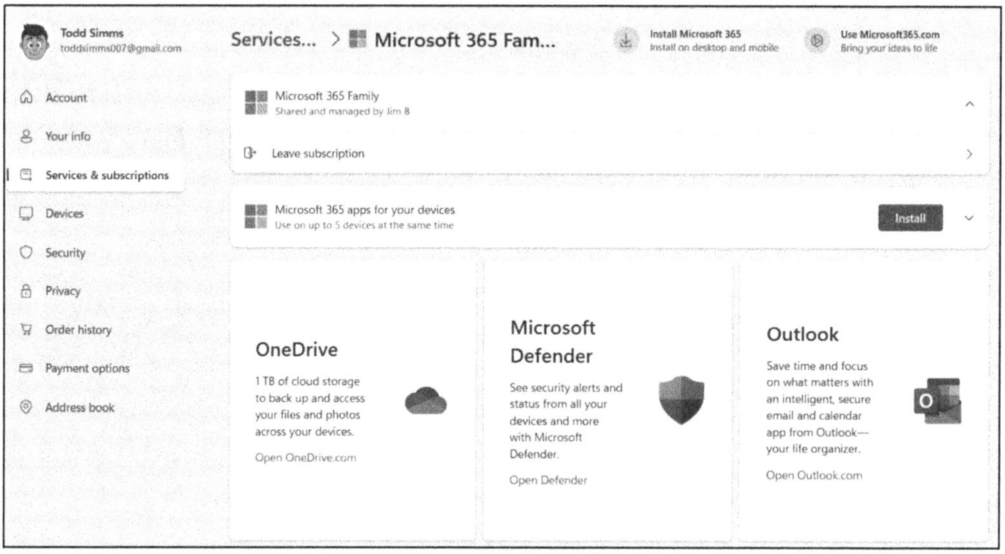

Figure 6.12

You may want to check out some of the other sections under your account settings to make sure everything looks correct.

Getting Help

Just like with any other app you might use, there will be a time when you cannot figure something out or find that something doesn't seem to be working the way you think it should be. When this happens, you can try out the OneDrive help options to see if you can find an answer to your question.

OneDrive has a help feature that can be accessed by clicking on the question mark icon at the upper right corner of the page. This will then open a window with some suggested training topics as well as a search box where you can type in your question or details about your problem.

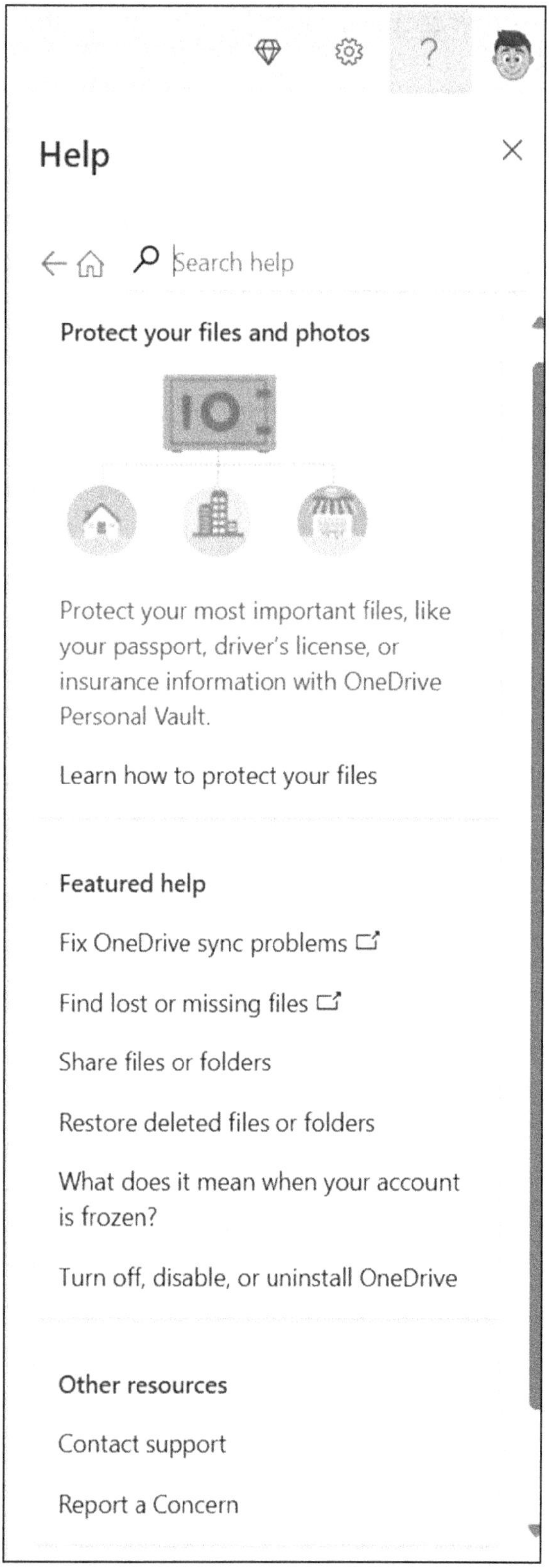
Help
Search help
Protect your files and photos
Protect your most important files, like your passport, driver's license, or insurance information with OneDrive Personal Vault.
Learn how to protect your files
Featured help
Fix OneDrive sync problems
Find lost or missing files
Share files or folders
Restore deleted files or folders
What does it mean when your account is frozen?
Turn off, disable, or uninstall OneDrive
Other resources
Contact support
Report a Concern
Figure 6.13

For example, if I were to type in "can't find my file," the help system would show me results related to my query. I can then click on one of these topics to read up on it and hope that it has the information I need.

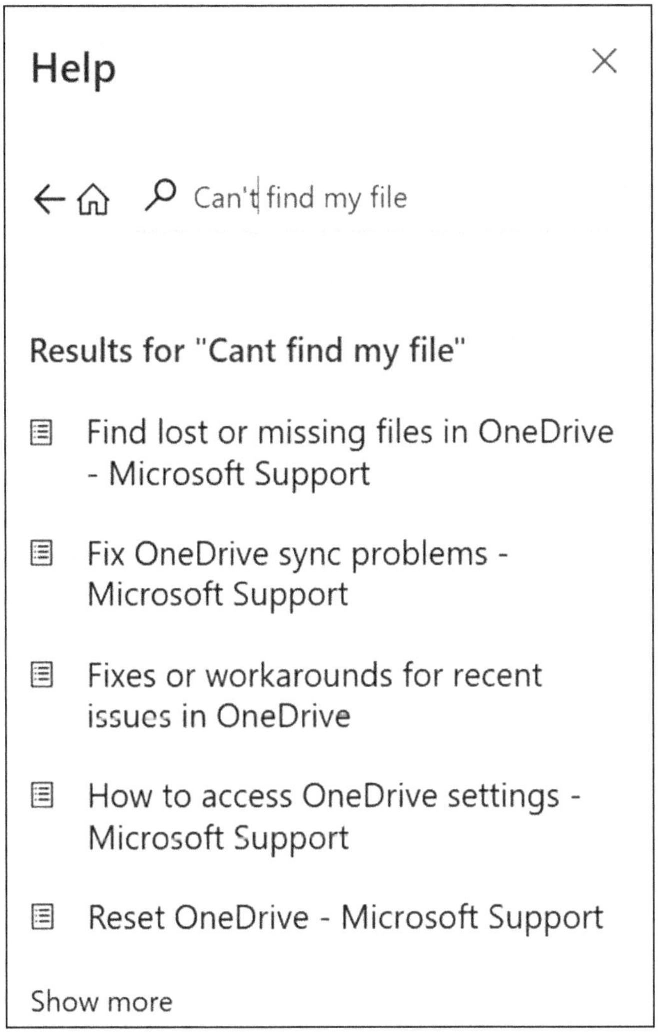

Figure 6.14

If you look back at Figure 6.13, you will see that there is a *contact support* option as well. When you type in your question here, you will also get suggested results that you can click on to see if they can help you out.

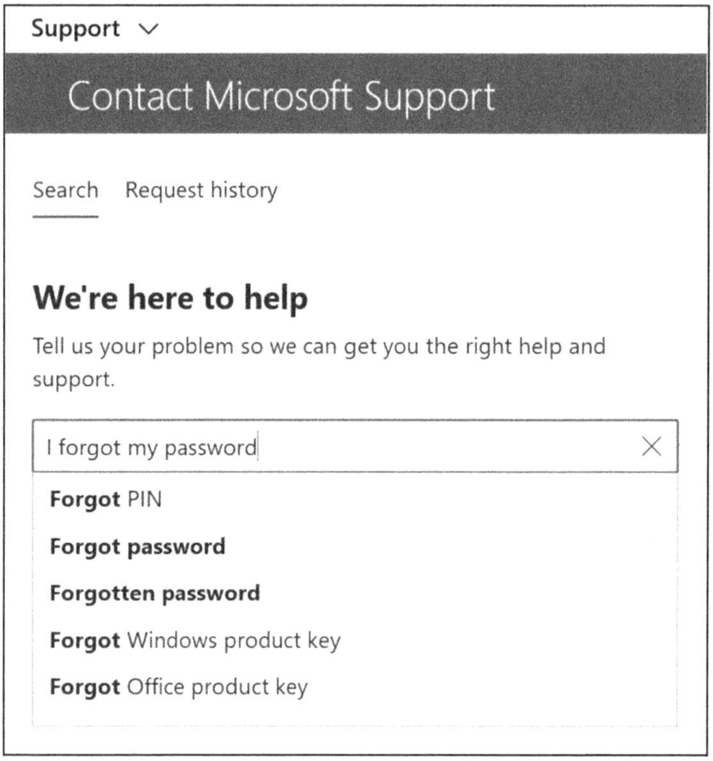

Figure 6.15

If you were to skip the suggestions, you can then click on the *Get Help* button for additional options.

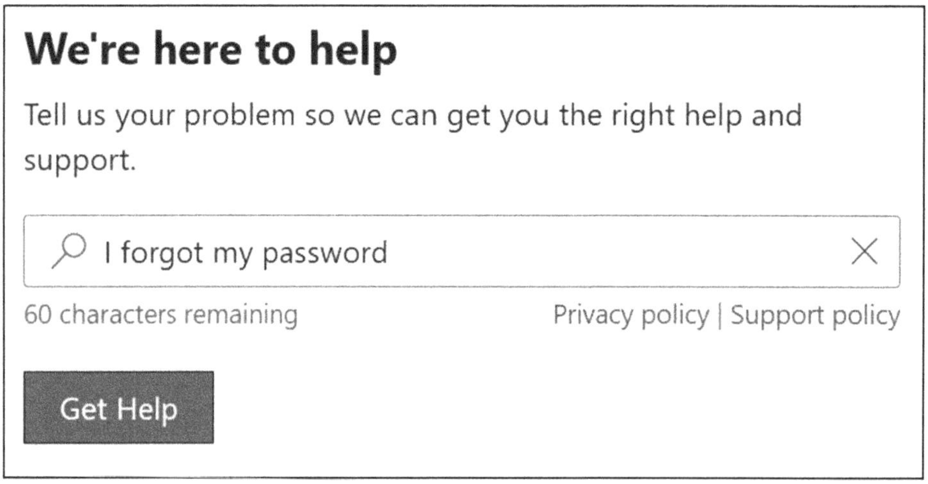

Figure 6.16

You will then see more suggested topics that you can click on. If none of the suggestions apply to your issue, then you should see a button at the bottom that says *Sign in to contact support*.

Here you will need to select a product that applies to your situation. Since OneDrive is not on the list, you can choose *Other Products*.

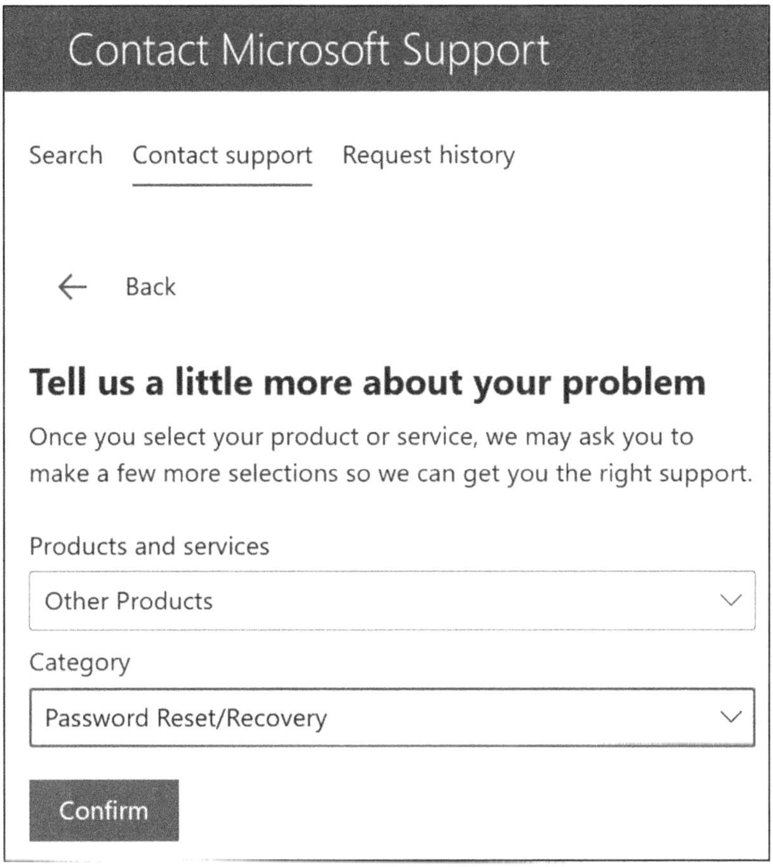

Figure 6.17

Here is where things can get a bit tricky. If you are using the free version of OneDrive without a Microsoft 365 account, then your support options will be very limited and your only option might be to go to the Microsoft forum and post your question there (Figure 6.18).

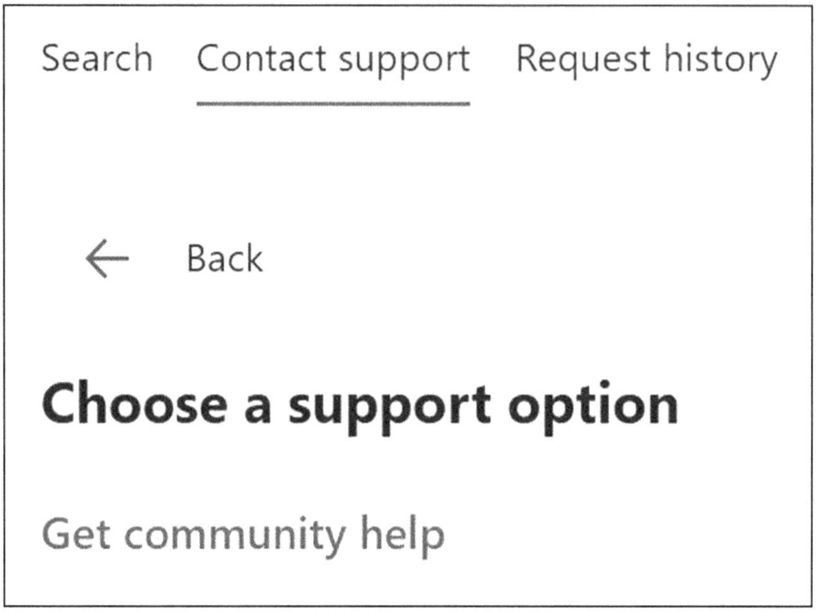

Figure 6.18

Figure 6.19 shows the same query using an account with a paid subscription.

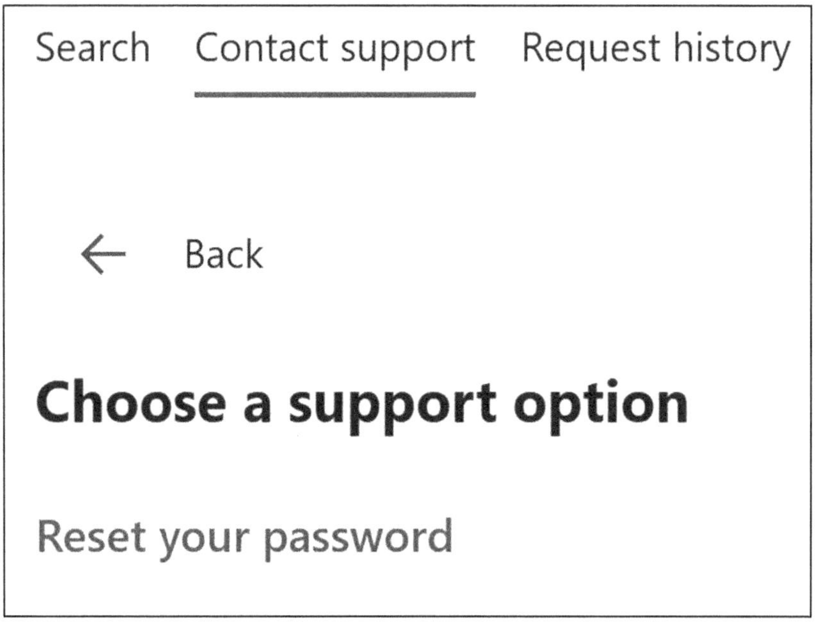

Figure 6.19

If I were to change the category and question type from Figure 6.17, I get the option to chat with a Microsoft support agent when using a subscription based account.

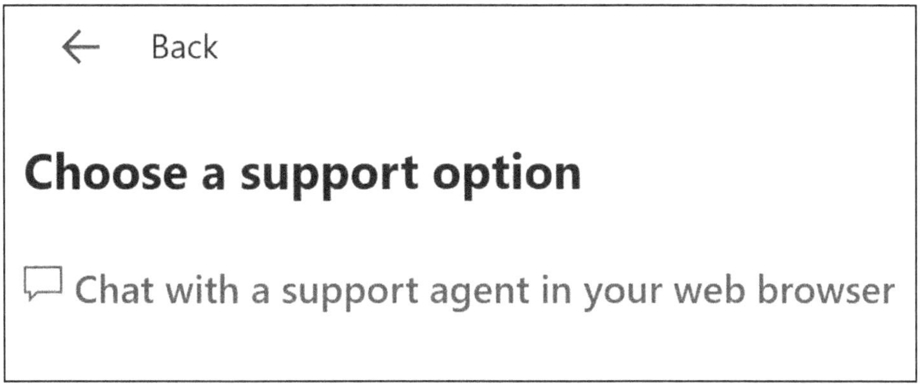
Back
Choose a support option
Chat with a support agent in your web browser

Figure 6.20

What’s Next?

Now that you have read through this book and taken your OneDrive skills to the next level, you might be wondering what you should do next. Well, that depends on where you want to go. Are you happy with what you have learned, or do you want to further your knowledge or try out some of the more advanced features that come with the Personal or Family plans?

If you do want to expand your knowledge on other cloud technology-related topics, you should look at subject-specific books such as cloud storage or hosted servers and services. Focus on one subject at a time, then apply what you have learned to the next subject. You can also check my other books that cover a wider range of topics mentioned above and then some.

There are many great video resources as well, such as Pluralsight or CBT Nuggets, which offer online subscriptions to training videos of every type imaginable. YouTube is also a great source for training videos if you know what to search for.

If you are content with being a OneDrive power user who knows more than your friends, then just keep on reading up on the technologies you want to learn, and you will soon become your friends and family's go-to computer person, which may or may not be something you want!

Thanks for reading **Microsoft OneDrive Made Easy**. You can also check out the other books in the Made Easy series for additional computer-related information and training. You can get more information on my other books on my Computers Made Easy Book Series website.

https://www.madeeasybookseries.com

COMPUTERS MADE EASY
WINDOWS 10 MADE EASY
NETWORKING MADE EASY
CLOUD STORAGE MADE EASY
GOOGLE APPS MADE EASY
OFFICE MADE EASY
ANDROID SMARTPHONES MADE EASY
THE INTERNET MADE EASY
WINDOWS HOME NETWORKING MADE EASY
BUILDING YOUR OWN COMPUTER MADE EASY
PHOTOSHOP ELEMENTS MADE EASY
POWERPOINT MADE EASY
PUBLISHER MADE EASY
PREMIERE ELEMENTS MADE EASY
VIRTUALBOX MADE EASY
ZOOM MADE EASY
GOOGLE MEET MADE EASY
SLACK MADE EASY
GOOGLE CLASSROOM MADE EASY
GOOGLE DOCS MADE EASY
GOOGLE SITES MADE EASY
MICROSOFT OFFICE FOR THE WEB MADE EASY
WIX MADE EASY
WINDOWS VIDEO EDITOR MADE EASY
COMPUTERS FOR SENIORS MADE EASY
GMAIL MADE EASY
WINDOWS 11 FILE MANAGEMENT MADE EASY
WINDOWS 11 MADE EASY
SOCIAL MEDIA FOR SENIORS MADE EASY
EMAIL FOR SENIORS MADE EASY
DROPBOX MADE EASY
WINDOWS 11 FOR SENIORS MADE EASY
ONENOTE MADE EASY
ANDROID SMARTPHONES FOR SENIORS MADE EASY
WINDOWS MAIL AND CALENDAR MADE EASY
GOOGLE DRIVE MADE EASY
THE INTERNET FOR SENIORS MADE EASY
GOOGLE PHOTOS MADE EASY
VMWARE WORKSTATION MADE EASY
CLIPCHAMP VIDEO EDITOR MADE EASY
MICROSOFT SWAY MADE EASY
BOX MADE EASY
MICROSOFT WORD FOR SENIORS MADE EASY
GOOGLE FORMS MADE EASY
CANVA MADE EASY
MICROSOFT EXCEL FUNDAMENTALS MADE EASY
OUTLOOK FOR WINDOWS MADE EASY
MICROSOFT OUTLOOK FOR SENIORS MADE EASY
JAMES BERNSTEIN

You should also check out my computer tips website, as well as follow it on Facebook to find more information on all kinds of computer topics. I also have online training courses you can take at your own pace.

www.onlinecomputertips.com
https://www.facebook.com/OnlineComputerTips/
http://madeeasytraining.com

About the Author

James Bernstein has been working with various companies in the IT field for over 20 years, managing technologies such as SAN and NAS storage, VMware, backups, Windows Servers, Active Directory, DNS, DHCP, Networking, Microsoft Office, Exchange, and more.

He has obtained certifications from Microsoft, VMware, CompTIA, ShoreTel, and SNIA, and continues to strive to learn new technologies to further his knowledge on a variety of subjects.

He is also the founder of the website onlinecomputertips.com, which offers its readers valuable information on topics such as Windows, networking, hardware, software, and troubleshooting. Jim writes much of the content himself and adds new content on a regular basis. The site was started in 2005 and is still going strong today.